CELTIC
SAINTS
and
THEIR
ANIMAL
FRIENDS

A Spiritual
Kinship

CELTIC SAINTS and THEIR ANIMAL FRIENDS

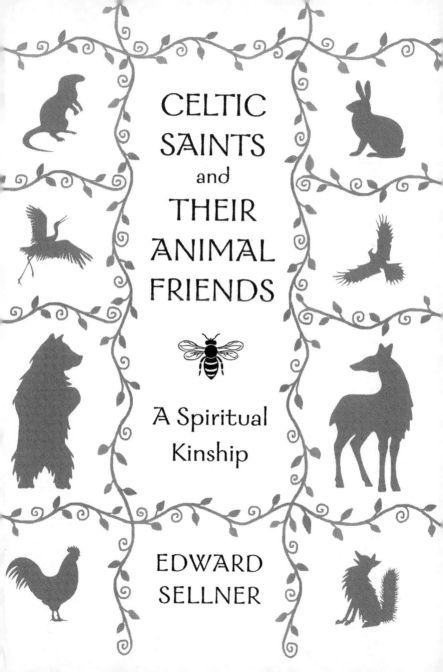

A Spiritual Kinship

EDWARD SELLNER

Anamchara Books
Vestal, New York 13850
www.anamcharabooks.com

paperback ISBN: 978-1-62524-903-6
eBook ISBN: 978-1-62524-904-3

CONTENTS

Introduction	7
1. Patrick of Armagh	51
2. Brigit of Kildare	57
3. Columcille of Iona	65
4. Brendan of Clonfert	73
5. Ciaran of Saighir	85
6. Colman of Kilmacduagh	93
7. Columban of Luxeuil	97
8. Cuthbert of Lindisfarne	103
9. David of Wales	111
10. Gall of Saint Gallen	119
11. Gobnait of Ballyvourney	127
12. Godric of Finchale	133
13. Ita of Killeedy	141
14. Kevin of Glendalough	147
15. Maedoc of Ferns	153
16. Melangell of North Powys	159
17. Modomnoc of Ossory	165
18. Ninian of Whithorn	171
19. Petroc of Padstow	175
20. Samthann of Clonbroney	181
Conclusion	185
Bibliography	197
About the Author	203

For Andrew and Clair Linzey

and

Red, my teacher and muse

Introduction

FROM ANCIENT TO MODERN TIMES, INDIGE-
nous peoples have long had a deep spiritual awareness that
all things are related to one another, and we are intrinsically
linked with Gaia, our mother Earth. As the phenomenon of
global climate change is increasingly making clear, when we
harm her, we harm ourselves. Native Americans, including
those who live in my part of the world, Minnesota, have long
had this sense of reality and fostered it in their daily lives and
spirituality. The Lakota phrase *mitakuye oyasin*—"all my rel-
atives"—said repeatedly in their ceremonies, is an affirma-
tion that we are connected with everyone and everything: not
only with those people who travel with us on our pilgrimage
through time but also with animals who often act as teachers,
healers, and guides. This awareness was shared with the ancient

Celts of Ireland, Scotland, Wales, the Isle of Man, Cornwall in England, Brittany in France, and Galicia in Spain, a perspective they passed on to those early Celtic Christians who built monasteries that eventually grew into a form of Christianity much different from the one influenced by the dominant Roman culture that arose on the continent of Europe. A sense of kinship with animals and all creation became a major characteristic of Celtic Christian spirituality.

This book focuses on this sense of kinship as reflected in the stories of the Celtic saints. By presenting these stories, I hope that you, the reader, will begin to recognize, if you haven't already, the significance of this quality of kinship, and that you will go on to affirm its importance in your own life.

It is an aspect of my spiritual heritage I had overlooked in my earlier research on those saints, even though I grew up in rural North Dakota where cattle, sheep, pigs, and chickens, as well as cats and dogs, were familiar sights and, at times, intimate friends. As I grew older, however, certain experiences made me more aware of this kinship between humans, animals, and birds: when I observed, for example, on my first visit to Lindisfarne, the Holy Isle off the northern coast of England, the Anglican priest there communing with his dog, and how she seemed to reciprocate, the two of them sharing a secret language; how crows gathered in my neighbor's tree across the street from my home back in Minnesota, turning the tree into a living mass of blackness on the day my neighbor, a man of Irish ancestry, died; how, at my father's burial, my aunt exclaimed aloud at all the birds filling the trees and telephone lines, seeming to have come to the country cemetery to mourn my father, a man who had fed so many of them while he was alive. Also, I was raised with various puppies and dogs; my father gave me my first one, Peppy, at Christmas when I was almost five years old, amazing me with this unexpected bundle of energy and affection. More recently, when my dear cocker spaniel, Red, died after months of lingering illness, I reaffirmed once more how much happiness certain pets bring into our daily lives. In the midst of my deep grieving, Red's loving spirit still accompanies me—even though her ashes are buried in my backyard, beneath a Celtic cross, visible from my kitchen window.

When we turn to the stories of the Celtic saints, we find numerous affirmations of this spiritual kinship and the affection found between these saints and the animals they loved, who loved them. If we pay close attention, if we practice a form of meditation Buddhists call mindfulness, we can begin to learn from these stories how to better live our daily lives, behave more compassionately toward all our fellow earthlings, and be more appreciative of what animals give us so freely and generously as guides into a richer humanity.

To more fully understand and appreciate the wisdom that the stories of the Celtic saints and their animal friends provide, let us first consider the saints' ancestors, the ancient Celts, whose spiritual leaders taught them about their mystical connection with Nature and with their fellow creatures. When we consider the history, culture, and spirituality of the ancient Celts, we find stories of animals everywhere we turn.

A Celtic Perception of the World

In the history of Western civilization, the Celts have, until quite recently, received little attention, largely because, unlike the Greeks and Romans, they did not write anything down until the sixth century CE, when Christian scribes adapted the Latin alphabet for writing their native Celtic languages. Before that, all the Celts' history, knowledge, and lore were kept alive through the oral tradition of the bards, the story-tellers, and other learned members of the tribes.

Modern archaeologists are finding, however, that, even before the rise of the Roman Empire, the Celts, a branch of the Indo-European family from which most of present-day European, Middle Eastern, and Indian peoples are descended, dominated the center of Europe for centuries, from the Black Sea to Spain, and from the Mediterranean to the North Sea and Ireland. More archaeological evidence of the Celts' talents and sophistication, such as advanced agricultural techniques and the craftsmanship and metalwork that have survived, clearly demonstrates the scale and importance of the Celtic contribution to the formation of European civilization. The names of many major cities in modern Europe, such as Paris, Milan, Vienna, London, and Berlin, trace their origin to the Celts, as do the names of such rivers as the Thames, the Seine, the Rhine, and the Danube. In England, the cities of Bath and Wells were originally holy Celtic sites where the thermal waters were used for bathing and making offerings to Celtic deities. Even the site of the beautiful medieval Chartres Cathedral in France was once a main Celtic center, where spiritual leaders, the druids and druidesses, are said to have met annually.

The precise geographical origins of the Celtic race are unclear. Some scholars point to the area near India, while others say that Celtic civilization emerged around 700 BCE in the Hallein region of Austria, where the Bronze-Age "Hallstatt Culture" was born. Another location, discovered by archaeologists at La Tene on Lake Neuchatel in Switzerland, points to the presence of Celts there around the early fifth century BCE. The burial mounds at both places have produced many artifacts and images that reveal a people who imported luxury goods, especially drinking equipment, from the Mediterranean world, and who appreciated abstract designs in their art, which incorporated motifs from Nature, such as animals, birds, and foliage, as well as human faces—a trait which appears much

later in the most famous of illuminated Christian Gospels, the
Book of Kells, created around 800 CE.

Wherever their actual beginnings, we know the ancient
Celts engaged in a great variety of occupations: warriors,
farmers, adventurers, traders, and craftsmen. They were also
a nomadic people, given to travel and migration. Wherever
they went, they brought with them a certain Celtic perception
of the world, reflected in their admiration for poetry and the
arts, their strong sense of the intimate connection between
this world and the next, their belief in the sacredness of landscape, their experience of ongoing communion between the
living and the dead—and, not least, their veneration of Nature
in all its manifestations. These qualities of the ancient Celts
persisted, even after the coming of Christianity.

From the fifth through the third centuries BCE, Celtic
tribes moved south into northern Italy, west through Gaul
and Iberia, east along the Danube into Hungary, Greece,
Turkey, and across the North Sea into Britain. By about 387
BCE, they had grown so powerful that some of them sacked
Rome itself, and by 279 BCE, they attacked the Greek oracle
at Delphi. Much of Gaul (present-day France) before Caesar's
invasions in the 50s BCE, contained Celtic tribes.

Under the Roman emperors Augustus and Tiberius,
the remainder of Celtic Europe was subdued. In 43 CE, the
conquest of Britain was initiated, and by 84 CE, Roman armies

reached northern Scotland. Only Ireland remained unconquered by the power of Rome.

Due to conflicts with other tribes, including the Anglo-Saxons who invaded Britain in the fifth century CE, and because of their own desire to be near bodies of water, Celtic tribes eventually settled in those places we now associate with the insular lands, the "Celtic Fringe": Ireland, Scotland, Wales, the Isle of Man, Cornwall in England, Brittany in France, and Galicia in Spain. During Christian times, monks and missionaries from Ireland, as well as Iona off the coast of Scotland, passed Celtic spirituality on to the Anglo-Saxons in Northumbria (northern England), as well as the continent of Europe, especially the lands we know today as France, Germany, Switzerland, and Italy.

The Natural Environment of Celtic Landscape

The ancient Celts' daily life was lived in close proximity to Nature, and their spirituality reflected what the Welsh call *hud*: a sense of wonder and awe at the Divine residing in everything. Their ancestors, like other indigenous peoples, had a deep respect for Nature, regarding the Earth as a mother, the source of all fertility. Their spiritual leaders believed that what we think of as the "supernatural" pervaded every aspect of life, and that spirits were everywhere: in trees and sacred groves, mountaintops and rock formations, rivers, streams, and holy wells.

Influenced by that ancient spiritual heritage, Celtic Christians found it natural to address God as "Lord of the Elements" or "God of the cloudy skies" or "Lord of the starry night," and to experience communion with God in their natural surroundings. In the stories of the saints, they are often found establishing their monasteries and oratories in places where the druids and druidesses had once taught and worshipped: in the midst of oak groves or near sacred springs, on the shores of secluded lakes, or on misty islands far out at sea.

Before the saints and soul friends of the Celtic church, even before the rise of the Celts whom later Christian generations identified as "Pagan," the land and the ocean that borders it was there. This landscape—its mountains covered with forests and flowers, its tiny islands and skellig rocks off the shores of lakes and seas, the ocean water with its ebb and flow of tides—shaped the Celts' innate appreciation of beauty. This natural loveliness, wreathed so often in mists and fogs, opened the Celts, both ancient and Christian, to the realm of the imagination. It made them receptive to mysticism, poetry, and prayer, as well as to the mysterious language and images of dreams.

Located as they were so close to the ocean, the lands of the Celts were watered almost daily by mists and sudden downpours of rain. This weather, which changes so quickly and unexpectedly from bright sunshine to the blackest of days, also contributed to the Celts' temperament, their outlook on life, their character. The early twentieth-century poet and folklorist Kenneth MacLeod described the Celt as "a creature of extremes; his sadness is despairing, his joy is rapture."

The same changing weather may also have contributed to the Celts' penchant for telling stories. As Irish playwright Bryan MacMahon once said in answer to a student's query about the flood of Celtic stories, "Oh, it's the rain you know. It turns one to moody reflection, and what else can you do of a long winter's night but tell stories." Certainly, Nature and the natural environment contributed to the writing of stories about the saints who were surrounded by the beauty of Nature and friendly animals.

Anyone who visits the lands associated with the Celts would agree they have a common landscape. Wake up in the morning, look out through the window, and, if you are near the sea, you realize how much they look alike: in springtime, you'll see green leaves returning to the trees, and fuchsia blossoming in rich colors of scarlet and creamy white; in summer, wild gorse bushes splash the fields and hills with patches of bright yellow, as if from the brush of van Gogh; in autumn, the tops of mountains and hills are encircled with various shades of tan, blue, and purple heather; in winter, cold rain sweeps in sheets across rugged rock formations and deserted beaches. And always, there is the sense of the sea, its vast expanse of water, its ever-changing crests of waves. Ruman, a seventh-century Irish poet, refers to the beauty and power of the ocean:

> *Full the sea and fierce the surges,*
> *Lovely are the ocean verges,*
> *On the showery waters whirling,*
> *Sandy winds are swiftly swirling,*
> *Rudders cleave the surf that urges.*

For the ancient Celts, a people who have been described in sometimes highly condescending terms such as "mere animists," the landscape was inhabited by multitudes of spirits and by goddesses and gods of Nature and of fertility. When Christianity came to Celtic lands, this profound belief in the spiritual dimension of creation was transformed into the Christian belief in the spiritual presence and ready accessibility of God, the angels, and the saints, all of whom, from a Celtic perspective, were not divorced from but closely linked with the environment. A story about Saint Columcille alludes to this powerful sense of spiritual presence, relating why he loved his Irish monastery at Derry so much, located high on the hill where the city by that name was later built:

> *For this is the reason why I love Derry,*
> *For its level fields, for its brightness,*
> *Because it is quite full of white angels*
> *From one end to the other. . . .*
> *My Derry, my little oak-grove,*
> *My dwelling, my little cell.*

For Columcille and other Celts, ancient and Christian, landscape was both *luminous*, overflowing with light, and *numinous*, reveling in and revelatory of sacred mystery. Contrary to those of us who live in a culture that has lost its memory and seems to only value the future and the supposedly ever-changing "new," the Celts believed the landscape itself was filled with echoes of both memory and the eternal, alive with the continuing presence of past lives. The Irish writer John Synge alludes to this when he says the Celts believe in a "psychic memory" attached to the landscape and its locales.

The Celts brought this awareness to the landscape, and their attitude toward it was one of wonder and awe at its profound beauty and effulgence. Irish theologian Noel Dermot O'Donoghue refers to this as "Celtic religious consciousness, Christian as well as pre-Christian," in which "creation does not merely show forth God's glory," but "has its own power, its own presence, its own mystery, its own voices."

Influenced by this awareness of Nature's mystery, the Irish shared with their later invaders, the Norsemen, what the Norse called *utiseta,* the practice of sitting out under the moon and the stars to listen attentively to the voices of Nature: singing water, rustling leaves, birdcalls, and the constant murmur of the wind. As the ninth-century Irish scholar John Scotus Eriugena stated: "Every visible and invisible creature can be called a theophany, that is, an appearance of the Divine," a belief reflected centuries later in the Welsh poetry of Waldo Williams, who wrote about the "ancient kinship of earth and heaven."

Anyone who reads the stories of the Celtic saints or visits their holy places soon realizes the landscape is not merely "background" to the lives of these saintly soul friends, but a vital and formative presence, affecting profoundly their spirituality and their understanding of God. This theology is reflected in a medieval Irish litany to the Trinity that addresses God:

> *O Creator of the elements . . . ,*
> *O God of the earth,*
> *O God of fire.*
> *O God of the waters of wonder.*
> *O God of the gusting and blustering air. . . .*
> *O God of the waves from the depths of the ocean.*
> *O God of the planets and of the many bright stars.*

O God, creator of the universe and inaugurator
of night and day.

In the recognition of Nature's beauty in high places and ocean depths, in plant life and animal friends, Celts, both ancient and Christian, experienced a mystical connection with Nature. This sense of spiritual kinship is reflected in their profound respect for the Earth and the natural rhythms of body and soul. They did not see themselves as "lords" over creation, but spiritually, emotionally, and intellectually connected with it. Their daily lives and work were united with their landscape, as well as with the changing seasons of the year. Sun and moon, sea and lake, wind and fire, earth and sky, all have numinous associations in early Celtic literature, especially as seen in the poetry of the Nature mystics and solitaires.

The Ancient Celts' Mystical Connection with Animals

This attitude of deep respect for the environment was manifest in the Celts' quiet care for all living things. As we will see in their stories, the Celtic saints seem to have had a special affinity with animals in relationships that were reciprocated: Kevin shelters in his hands a blackbird that probably sang for him; Ciaran meets a wild boar who helps him clear land for his monastery; Columcille's white horse sheds great tears at his master's approaching death. Animals are portrayed as fellow creatures of the Earth, and, once befriended, they become the saints' helpers and companions.

Like many shamans throughout history, ancient Celtic druids and druidesses knew from firsthand experience of the mystical connection between humans and animals. Animals, in fact, were considered helping spirits who guided not only the spiritual leaders of the tribes but also ordinary people through life's conflicts and difficulties, sometimes helping them attain a new direction in life or a new identity. Certain animals were considered to be "psychopomps," spiritual guides for the living who also guide the souls of the dead into the next world. For both the living and the dead, an animal could provide very real contact with the spiritual world. Animals often served as guides to the Celts' "thin places," geographical sites where a person could experience "the thin veil" between this world and the next.

Celtic legends of their heroes had much in common with those found in other lands where the hero is led by animals to new lands and new awareness. In numerous instances, helping animals not only enables a person to be transformed, but an animal may also become the individual's "double," an alter ego, another self waiting to be born. This is particularly evident, for example, in North America's Indigenous people, who name themselves after animals such as Black Elk, Crazy

Horse, Sitting Bull, Lone Wolf, and Kicking Bear. In a similar way, the ancient Celts not only gave individual families the names of animals—such as McMahon, which translates as "Son[s] of the Bear"—but a number of tribes also took the names of animals whose attributes they admired, such as the Epidii of Kintyre (Horse-People), the Lugi in Sutherland (People of the Raven), the Caerini (People of the Sheep), the Orcoi (Boar People—whose name still lives on in the Orkney Isles), Gamandrad (Stork People), and others.

The Celts' sense of kinship with animals is also manifest in the tales of their deities and heroes, most of whom had animal or bird companions, while many were also associated with shape-shifting. The ancient god Cernunnos, Lord of the Animals, was portrayed as half human, half animal, wearing on his head the antlers of a stag. CuChulainn, the Irish hero who appears in many Irish, Scottish, and Manx folktales, was called "the Hound of Culann" and had a special and close relationship with dogs. Finn McCool, another hero and hunter-warrior of Irish, Scottish, and Manx mythology, was known as someone who would pass through many shapes of animals and birds. His wife, Sava, is part deer and part woman; the first time CuChulainn meets her, she is in the shape of a fawn, having been transformed by a druid's magic. Her son, Oisin, whose name means "Little Deer," is described as half-fawn, half-child. (Celtic tradition has many deer stories; one of the earliest

Christian tales has Saint Patrick changing himself and his men into deer in order to hide from a pursuing chieftain.) The sixth-century Welsh shaman-poet Taliesin is said to have transformed himself into numerous animals, including a snake, eagle, sow, crane, cat, goat, salmon, dog, fox, and squirrel—much like the Buddha's hundreds of previous incarnations, many as animals, before his birth as Gautama.

Animals play prominent roles in numerous ancient stories.

- Wolves, for example, appear in many of these tales, often associated with Morrigan, the battle goddess of the Celts, as well as the Irish king, Cormac MacAirt, who was kidnapped as a child and reared by a she-wolf before he was found and returned to his mother. (In the lives of the saints, we find two of them—Ailbe, an Irish saint, and Ciwa, a Welsh saint—were suckled by wolves as children, much as the legendary founders of Rome, Romulus and Remus, were said to have been.)

- Deer, especially stags, appear frequently in Celtic literature, as they also do in the later stories of the saints who are most often depicted as protecting them from hunters. Interestingly, some of the ancient

Celtic stories tell of a gigantic deer-goddess, whose chariot was drawn by four golden-antlered deer.

- Pigs and wild boars in the ancient tales are often portrayed as magical beings with oracular powers that allow them to foretell the future. The most famous sow, Hen Wen (Old White One), was said to have acquired great knowledge from eating the beech nuts that fell from the Tree of Wisdom.

- Otters, called "water-dogs," were considered lucky. In the story of the hero Muiredach, he kills the King of the Otters and then wears its skin as a mantle that protects him.

- Numerous stories of cats appear in Celtic folklore, some of them about large black cats, associated with fairies and witches, similar to those depicted today at Halloween. In the immram story the *Voyage of Maelduin* (a predecessor of the *Voyage of Saint Brendan*), the hero and his men discover on one of the islands where they land a seemingly harmless little kitten—who suddenly changes into a flaming arrow, killing one of Maelduin's men when he is about to steal a piece of jewelry. Some ancient Celts, notably in southeastern Wales, worshipped a cat;

and in Scotland, some of the natives called themselves "Cats." Early Irish literature refers to *Inse Catt*, the Isles of the Cats. And perhaps the most famous of Irish cats is Pangur Bán, whose ninth-century human companion penned these lines:

> *I and Pangur Bán, my cat,*
> *'Tis a like task we are at;*
> *Hunting mice is his delight,*
> *Hunting words I sit all night. . . .*
>
> *Oftentimes a mouse will stray*
> *In the hero Pangur's way;*
> *Oftentimes my keen thought set*
> *Takes a meaning in its net. . . .*
>
> *When a mouse darts from its den,*
> *O! how glad is Pangur then;*
> *O! what gladness do I prove*
> *When I solve the doubts I love.*
>
> *So in peace our task we ply,*
> *Pangur Bán, my cat, and I;*
> *In our arts we find our bliss,*
> *I have mine, and he has his.*

Cats thus were very popular among the Celts—similar to Asian people's love of them. In Japan, for example, there are many shrines and temples, even an island, dedicated to cats and cat deities, and Buddhist monasteries in Myanmar and Thailand specifically care for cats, who are treated as fellow monks (as we will see was the case in stories of Celtic saints and their animal-friends).

- Dogs too, of course, are found in Celtic stories, some of whom we know by name, including King Arthur's great hound Cafall and Finn McCool's dog Bran. Many Celtic heroes and kings include the appellation "hound," as we saw with CuChulainn, showing their love of and identity with dogs. Irish folklore describes three amazing green dogs named Fios, Luaths, and Tron (Knowledge, Swiftness, and Heaviness)—which seems appropriate on the Emerald Isle!

- Birds also often appear in the ancient tales. Crows and ravens are depicted as bringers of knowledge, and cranes were much loved by the Irish. Perhaps the most famous story is that of the Crane of Moy Leana, who, weary and lonesome, is saved by Aengus Mac Orc (much as Saint Columcille would do for a poor, weary crane seeking refuge on Iona). Swans, considered by the Celts to be Otherworldly birds, also figure frequently in Celtic stories, especially those associated with the Ulster hero CuChulainn and the love-god Aengus Og. Perhaps the most famous story of swans is the one about the Children of Lir who were turned into swans by their jealous stepmother, remaining swans for three hundred years before finally returning to human form. (In the beautiful Garden of Remembrance in Dublin, dedicated to those who gave their lives for the cause of Irish freedom, the sculpture depicts the children of Lir being transformed from swans into children once again.)

So many of the stories about animals in Celtic mythology show them to have special powers. The salmon was especially revered, for example, and the Celts believed that when eaten, the salmon would bestow a deep knowledge or wisdom. As in a considerable number of myths and legends from all over the world, the Celtic hero is often portrayed as being carried into the beyond or into another stage of life by an animal. In many cultures' traditions, the fox, the owl, the bear, the dog (and in Hawaii, the shark) are powerful and effective helpers.

Encounters with animal guides and spirits, Celts believed, happen at crossroads or liminal places: at twilight, for example, or deep within a dark wood, at the water's edge, or high upon a hill—in "thin places" where only a translucent film divides this world and the next, geographical locations where past, present, and future merge, and different worlds and species come together and interact for their mutual benefit. A Celtic proverb refers to these mysterious, mesmerizing places: "Heaven and earth are only three feet apart, but in thin places that distance is even shorter."

All these stories and traditions bear witness to the central belief of the Celts that wisdom is derived from friendship with animals and the rest of Nature. The stories of the Celtic saints emerged from still more ancient stories that were told in tribal circles and around flaming hearths long before Christianity arrived on Celtic shores. These, the earliest Celtic stories involving animals, were verbally passed on from generation to generation by the bards, the storytellers of the ancient Celts, before they were compiled and written down in the early Christian period of the sixth century by the monastic scribes.

Artistic Depictions of Kinship with Animals

This fascination and admiration for animals is also revealed in early Celtic art's images and symbols of animals, particularly the Celts' metalwork and jewelry; bulls, boars, deer, and wolves were favorite subjects, but human and animal forms were often mixed in their artistry: a human face or head, for example, may have the ears of an animal or horns. Statues of Celtic divinities often show them accompanied by animals, most often bulls, boars, deer, wolves, and horses, and birds such as the raven. This is perhaps most beautifully expressed artistically in the famous Gundestrup cauldron, created about 100 BCE., where the god Cernunnos is depicted seated cross-legged, with tall antlers on his head, while holding a giant snake in one hand and a Celtic torc in the other, surrounded by numerous animals such as stags, dogs, and even a dolphin with a human rider!

Celtic iconography represents animals as equal to their gods and goddesses, unlike the Roman classical tradition that always depicted them as subordinate. Celtic visual art, like its stories, expresses a sense of mutuality and equality between Nature and the animal world and the human and spiritual or Divine realms. No rigid barriers exist between human and animal forms.

This sense of equality between humans and animals is vividly portrayed in later medieval churches. The portal archway, for example, of a medieval monastic church at Dysert O'Dea in Ireland shows twelve human and seven animal heads intermixed with each other, expressing what we today would call "cross-speciesism." On the doorway of Clonfert Cathedral at the site of a monastery founded by Saint Brendan in 554, even more human and animal heads are visible. In another part of Ireland, at Cormac's Chapel on the Rock of Cashel, numerous mysteriously carved heads, appearing to be both human and animal, decorate one of the archways. On a tympanum over the main door, a centaur, a mythological creature with the upper body of a human and the lower body and legs of a horse, is depicted shooting arrows at a huge lion. Again, there is this physical mixing of human and animal forms.

Reflecting this ancient Celtic appreciation of animals, numerous Christian high crosses of Ireland, Cornwall, Wales, Northern England, the Isle of Man, and Scotland are filled with depictions of animals, wild and tame, familiar and foreign. There, on these distinctively beautiful stone crosses, in the midst of multiple carvings of scriptural heroes from both Hebrew and Christian scriptures, as well as Desert Fathers and Celtic saints, are animals—deer, ducks, dogs, and cats. Even a camel and lions—hardly common creatures in Celtic lands—can be seen on a high cross in Drumcliff, Ireland. Other crosses in Ireland are rich with animal scenes:

- On the Kells Market Cross, a dog lies at the feet of a man bearing a long staff. Processing before them, from right to left, are a large bird with open wings, a frog, a fawn, a young bull, a boar, and two fine stags with spreading antlers.

- On another Kells cross, a dog runs alongside two horsemen mounted on steeds. (The people and monks at Kells must have had an appreciation of dogs!)

- On a cross at Castledermot are figures of two men who are hunting or herding a hare, deer, pig or boar, and a bird.

- At Ahenny, the site of the earliest Irish high crosses, one cross has a scene of animals that fills most of the base, which also shows a man standing under what appears to be a palm tree. Scholars interpret this as Adam in the Garden of Eden naming the beasts, since a palm tree often indicates a scene of Paradise.

- At Monasterboice, on Muiredach's high cross (one of the finest pieces of early medieval sculpture in Ireland) is a panel depicting two Desert Fathers, Anthony and Paul of Thebes, holding a loaf of bread with a raven on the ground beside them. Two cats, one with a kitten, the other with a bird, sit in high relief on the lowest part of the shaft.

These are just a few of the many high crosses in Ireland with animals carved on them in stone. Scotland's high crosses also have numerous animals, birds, fish, and men on horseback—as do those in Northumbria, England, the Isle of Man, and Wales.

The illuminated Gospels from the later Christian centuries are also alive with animal imagery. The pages of the most famous, the Book of Kells (now on view at Trinity College, Dublin), are decorated with wrestling animals, writhing snakes, fluttering birds, and fish, cocks, and hens, all painted in bright colors of wine-red, indigo, yellow, emerald-green, and deep ocean-blue, in the midst of whirls, spirals, and geometric circles. Included in the many illustrations are an otter catching fish, a panther with a red tongue hanging out, cats (in individual and family groupings), mice that are tugging at or escaping with communion hosts, a hare biting a vine, a salmon, a greyhound, multicolored peacocks, a stag, a she-goat, a dove, and a wolf. A lion, eagle, and calf represent the three evangelists of the Gospels: a lion for Mark, an eagle for John, and a calf for Luke (while a human represents Matthew). Lions in the Book of Kells symbolize Christ (similar to Aslan in C. S. Lewis's Chronicles of Narnia). Many of these animals in the Book of Kells can also be found in two earlier illuminated Gospel books, the Book of Durrow (also at Trinity College) and the Lindisfarne Gospels (at the British Library in London).

Snakes are also prominent decorative elements in the Book of Kells. Though later synonymous with the Devil, during the early medieval period the snake was a common symbol of Christ's resurrection. (As the sixth-century church father Saint Isidore commented, "Snakes are said to live for a long time, because when they shed their old skin, they are said to shed their 'old age.'")

All these artistic depictions of animals reveal how deeply the Celts considered them to be fellow creatures with whom they shared a common life. The properties of animals—their speed, sharp hearing, keen sight, and for some, the ability to fly—elevated them in Celtic eyes; in some ways, animals were superior to humans. A peculiar rapport between humans and animals is depicted in these works of art, as well as a deep respect and admiration for animals having traits humans did not. This ancient understanding and love of animals—and all Creation—became the foundation of Celtic spirituality.

The Early Celtic Church:
Rural and Monastic

No one knows with certainty when Christianity arrived in the insular lands of Ireland, England, Scotland, Wales, Brittany, the Isle of Man, and Spain (all lands bordering the ocean or other bodies of water). Saint Patrick is perhaps the best-known of the missionaries who converted Ireland, but he certainly was not the only person to proclaim the good news of the gospel in

Celtic lands. Christianity came by many routes, spread through the influence of many ordinary Christians.

It may have come first to Gaul (France) from the Middle East where Jesus had lived to Rome, the heart of the Empire, where Peter and Paul preached the good news and were martyred. With the arrival of the Christian faith in Gaul, Britain, Ireland, and beyond, Celtic Christianity began to flourish in the early centuries from the mid-400s on, primarily in rural areas before the rise of cities. Monasteries arose that became towns and cities in themselves.

By 600 CE in Ireland alone, there were more than eight hundred monasteries, and many more were in other Celtic lands. What emerged in those lands where the Celts lived, and where Roman culture and institutions were not dominant, was a form of Christianity that functioned—in the way authority was used and decisions made—more like an inclusive circle than a pyramid. While the Roman church on the continent adapted the social structures of the Roman empire by dividing land into dioceses ruled by bishops, Celtic Christians adapted their family-oriented tribal structures to monastic communities, with abbots and abbesses as spiritual fathers and mothers, some of whom were married with families of their own, with or without bishops in their midst. Celtic monasteries were linked by the friendship between their communities through their abbots and abbesses, not through the jurisdiction of a hierarchy.

While the Roman church increasingly isolated women from ecclesial positions, influenced as it was by a culture that largely excluded women from civic and religious functions, many of the women in the early Celtic churches were recognized as having all the talents and spiritual authority as men. Stories of the Celtic women saints are particularly fascinating: Saint Ita hears confessions and forgives sins, Saint Samthann has a miraculous crozier or staff like that of a bishop, and Saint Brigit is ordained as bishop. This recognition of women's gifts was influenced by the ancient Celts, who granted women similar legal rights as men and allowed them to be tribal leaders, warriors, and spiritual leaders. All of this is alluded to in a ninth-century manuscript, *Catalogue of the Saints in Ireland*, which states that the early founders of the Celtic church "did not reject the service and society of women." Many of the women were leaders, like Saint Brigit, of monastic communities consisting of both women and men. These "double monasteries" were a normal feature of the earliest monastic life in Ireland and England. (They were also the first to be dissolved when Roman ecclesial authorities gained control.)

Another significant difference that affected the spirituality of Celtic Christians was their proximity to the natural environment. While the Roman church increasingly built its churches in urban areas, sometimes far removed from forests and lakes, the Celtic church, mostly rural, built monasteries and hermitages in solitary places, in secluded valleys and forests, on the banks of broad rivers, near cascading streams and ocean tides. These were the locations where Nature's inhabitants could be seen and their melodies heard throughout the day and night, where natural beauty could be enjoyed. As nineteenth-century British archeologist J. Romilly Allen suggested, "No one who has visited any considerable number of ancient Celtic ecclesiastical buildings can fail to have been struck by the care which the monks took in selecting sites where feelings of religious devotion might be intensified by the contemplation of all that is beautiful in nature." This same sentiment is experienced by those who visit the valley and lakes of Glendalough or look across the River Shannon at Clonmacnoise; who feel the ocean spray after climbing the rock formations at Giant's Causeway or watch the crashing waves at the Land's Ends in Cornwall, at Saint-Malo in Brittany, and on the coast outside Santiago de Compostela in Spain.

When twentieth-century Celtic historian Kenneth Jackson wrote about a certain Irish monk by the name of Suibhne Geilt, he evoked this idyllic world of natural beauty and solitude, surrounded by animals:

A lovely glen with a lovely green-gushing stream flowing precipitously down over the cliff, and a blessed spot there where there was a gathering of saints and very many righteous people, and many too were the fair and lovely trees there with heavy luxuriant fruit on that cliff; many also there were the sheltering ivy bushes, and heavy-headed apple trees bending to earth with the weight of their fruit and there were also on that cliff wild deer and hares and great heavy swine, and many too were the fat seals that used to sleep there on that cliff after coming out of the great sea beyond.

The seventh-century Irish monk and hermit Manchin of Liath spoke in his poetry of his deep desire for communion with his natural environment and its inhabitants:

> *I wish, O Son of the living God,*
> *Eternal ancient King,*
> *For a secret hut in the wilderness*
> *That it may be my dwelling....*
>
> *A beautiful wood close by*
> *Around it on every side*
> *For the nurture of many-voiced birds*
> *To shelter and hide it....*

This is the housekeeping I would get,
I would choose it without concealing,
Fragrant fresh leeks, hens,
Salmon, trout, bees. . . .

And for me to be sitting for a time
Praying to God in every place.

Christian Celts had an eye for beauty: the beauty of the body, of the soul, of friendship, of the natural environment.

Celtic Nature Mystics, Poets, and Solitaires

We see this intimacy with Nature and deep appreciation of its beauty reflected in the early writings of the Christian Nature poets, mystics, and hermits of Ireland and Wales who, like the twentieth-century Trappist monk and poet Thomas Merton, loved their hermitages or huts in the wilderness. Hundreds of Irish and Welsh poems have survived, poems that scholars compare to the Buddhist and Taoist Nature poets of China, Japan, Korea, and other parts of Asia. These Celtic Nature poets made constant reference to the presence of animals and birds in their landscapes. They were clearly attuned to the natural world, having developed powers of keen observation and attentive listening.

A virtual Peaceable Kingdom is expressed in one untitled Irish poem, attributed to a certain Deirdre, which could easily be describing the landscape around Glendalough, the monastic site of Saint Kevin, situated in an Irish mountain area, surrounded by two lakes:

> *Glen of fruits and fish and lakes,*
> *Peaked hill of lovely wheat. . . .*
> *Glen full of bees, of the long-horned wild oxen.*
>
> *Glen of cuckoos and thrushes and blackbirds,*
> *Precious is its cover to every fox;*
> *Glen full of wild garlic and watercress and woods,*
> *Of shamrock and flowers, leafy and twisting-crested.*
>
> *Sweet are the bellings of the brown-backed dappled deer*
> *Under the oakwood over the bare hill top,*
> *Gentle hinds that are timid*
> *Lying hidden in the great-treed glen.*
>
> *. . . a slumberous paradise for the badgers*
> *in their quiet burrows with their young. . . .*
>
> *Glen of the sleek brown round-faced otters*
> *That are pleasant and active in fishing,*
> *Many are the white-winged stately swans,*

> *And salmon breeding along the rocky brink.*
> *... chalk-white starry sunny glen.*

In these beautiful, haunting, magical poems, we find mention of "the lonesome cry of the eagle," "the murmur of otters," and "the talk of foxes." We find references to "tame swine, goats, boars, wild swine"; we find "mighty whales," surely like the whale by the name Jasconius in the stories of Saint Brendan, patron saint of whales and dolphins. In this Nature poetry, we find "hunting dogs and hounds," as we will see in Saint Melangell's story; we find reference to deer and "dappled red-breasted fawns," as in the story of Saint Patrick saving a doe and her fawn; we find allusions to "the music of the wolf pack at the end of the very cold night," as Saint Maedoc, a friend of wolves, must have heard in the area where he lived. In this poetry of Celtic solitaires and mystics we find reference to a crane that "screams over its crags," perhaps like the wearied one who landed on Iona, which Saint Columcille saved; the "brown round-faced otters" may have looked like those who warmed Saint Cuthbert after he spent nights praying in the cold waters off Lindisfarne. And, as in Saint Kevin's story about the blackbird he protected, we find a blackbird alluded to in another Nature poem:

> *The bird that calls from the willow,*
> *Lovely is its little beak with its clear call,*

The melodious yellow bill of the jet-black hardy bird;
A lively tune is sung, the blackbird's note.

The writers of Celtic poetry complained about the bitter cold of winters; they expressed their longing for spring, as well as their grief and prayers for the dead, "as if every dead person were a special friend." They wrote about their fear of Viking raids. But overall, their writing is filled with overwhelming tones of profound gratitude and great joy that were rooted in both the natural and spiritual worlds.

The hermit's life was one of ascetic simplicity, in imitation of the Desert Mothers and Fathers who had gone in search of holiness into the desert regions of Egypt, Syria, and Palestine, beginning in the third century CE. Celtic monks loved the stories about these heroic women and men, and they sought to imitate their ascetical lifestyle. Celtic hermits, in particular, who lived outside the monasteries, often ate and drank only what they found in the surrounding woods or what they could grow in their own gardens. They picked nuts and berries when in season, and ate vegetables from the garden.

Many of the hermits apparently practiced a vegetarian diet. One poem, for example, describes the landscape around the cell of Marbhan: "An excellent spring, a cup of noble water to drink"; "acorns, spare berries . . . a clutch of eggs, honey, produce of wild onions—God has sent it—sweet apples, red whortleberries, crowberries." In the *Life of Saint Brendan,* we hear of Barrinthus and his friends coming to an island hermit-monastery, where they were greeted lovingly by the brothers who lived there "in harmony in all things": "for no other food or drink was served there but the roots of herbs and the fruits of the trees, and drink of water to sate their thirst." The *Life of Saint Kevin of Glendalough* tells us that Kevin lived "without food but nuts of the wood and plants of the ground and pure water to drink." In a commentary on the *Life of Saint Ciaran of Saighir*, we find: "And this was his meal every night, a little barley bread and two roots of murathach [probably some sort of root vegetable] and spring water."

Kenneth Jackson says that the distinctive thing about this poetry is that, unlike other pastoral traditions, such as that of the early Greeks, the Irish hermits "lived so much among the wild creatures that they became almost one with them, almost brothers to them, as if they were hardly conscious that there was any distinction of genus." Jackson points out that this is especially clear in the ninth-century poem of the monk and his pet cat, Pangur Bán, which, along with so many other stories in the *Lives of the Saints*, demonstrates this quality of intimacy.

Continual prayer was the hermits' and anchorites' occupation; freedom from distractions, and peacefulness was the way of life they desired. In many ways, they were doing what the Celts called "soul-making," preparing for a happy death and eternal union with God. Their huts were meant to be places "where spears are not feared," and where they could live "without an hour of quarrel, without the noise of strife," with animals all around them. Twentieth-century Celtic scholar Robin Flower states that it was the poets' rich spirituality and inner life that made their poetry so powerful. "It was not only that these scribes and anchorites lived by the destiny of their dedication in an environment of wood and sea," he writes; "it was because they brought into that environment an eye washed miraculously clear by a continual spiritual exercise that they, first in Europe, had that strange vision of natural things in an almost unnatural purity." This quality of purity of heart is manifest in a poem by an anonymous hermit:

> *Over my head the woodland wall*
> *Rises; the ouzel [blackbird] sings to me;*
> *Above my booklet lined with words*
> *The woodland birds shake out their glee.*
>
> *That's the blithe cuckoo chanting clear*
> *In mantle grey from bough to bough!*
> *God keep me still! for here I write*
> *A scripture bright in great woods now.*

This is the poetry of the Nature mystics in the woods, reflecting a profound appreciation of Creation and its inhabitants, expressed too in the stories of the saints, including the *Life of Saint Declan of Ardmore*: "For he was in his own dear cell which he had built, himself for himself. It is between wood and water in a strait and secret spot on the sea's brink, and a clear stream flows by it from the wood to the sea, and trees gird it beautifully round about."

Twentieth-century Irish poet and novelist Patrick Kavanagh echoes this same sense of wonder in his book, *Tarry Flynn*, whose fictional hero is based upon Kavanagh's own life and mystical beliefs:

> *The simple, fantastic beauty of ordinary things growing—*
> *marsh-marigolds, dandelions, thistles, and grass.*

According to Kenneth Jackson, about the same time that this Nature poetry was being written, around the eighth through the tenth centuries, the stories of the Celtic saints were also being transcribed on sheets of vellum and parchment. Considering the ancient stories of the Celtic heroes and deities that preceded those of the saints, as well as the natural environment in which the Celts lived, it's no wonder that their thoughts and creative works focused on, as Kavanagh says, the "fantastic beauty of ordinary things."

For the Celtic saints, animals were friends, birds carried messages, waters sang, and tree branches broke into melodies. The ancient Celts' stories of their heroes, passed down orally from generation to generation by bards, were transformed with the arrival of Christianity on their shores into a new form of written literature—hagiography,

Storytellers of the Celtic Saints

Whether shared around a fire or on the pages of a manuscript or book, the Celts knew the tremendous wonder of story. For Christian Celts, nothing was better for teaching wisdom and spirituality than the stories of Jesus and the saints.

What some historians call "the golden age" in Celtic Christianity is associated with the early Celtic saints who lived primarily in the sixth and seventh centuries, founding monasteries and spreading Christianity to other lands as well as their own. This age was followed in the late seventh to the thirteenth centuries with the writing of their stories in hagiographies or "Lives."

Hagiography is the genre of writing, developed in the early church, specifically concerned with the lives and holiness of spiritual leaders in the churches. The term comes from two Greek words: *graphe*, which means "writing," and *hagoi*, "saintly, holy." The Christian storytellers who first wrote down the legends of the saints drew upon the rich oral traditions that had been kept alive for centuries, preceding any writing. While these stories cannot be considered historical in the strict sense that we understand that term today, they do provide insights into the historical context of the Celtic monastic communities. Perhaps most of all, they reveal the values the Celtic saints expressed in their lives.

Hagiographers primarily wrote the *Lives* because they believed the saints whose lives they described had something important to teach people about holiness, prayer, service, and union with God. Ultimately, these stories—like the Gospel stories of Jesus—were written to inspire later generations of Christians to lead a life reflecting the values of their original founder.

Although the Gospels themselves do not specifically allude to the presence of animals at Christ's birth, certainly the nativity narratives of the shepherds visiting him (Luke 2:8–20) and of the Wise Men paying homage (Matthew 2:1–12) would imply that sheep and possibly camels and donkeys would have accompanied them. Some apocryphal texts have an ox and donkey worshipping the Christ Child, while the earliest artistic depiction of the nativity in a fourth-century sarcophagus from Italy shows Baby Jesus flanked by the ox at his head and the donkey at his feet.

As an adult, before he begins his ministry, Jesus spends time in Nature, away from people, "alone except for wild animals" (Mark 1:12). Later, as he grieves over the fate of Jerusalem, he compares himself to a mother hen who wants to gather her chicks to protect them from harm (Matthew 23:37–39).

Animals who are helpful and friendly to humans are common in many cultures' folklore, but the *Lives* of the Celtic saints are unique in that they make these connections within the context of Christian life. Animals become helpers to the saints, sometimes even assisting them in building their monasteries or acting as spiritual guides. Frequently, the saints are portrayed as patrons and protectors of both wild and tame animals. As the scholar Charles Plummer said:

> Often does the saint interpose to save a hunted animal from its pursuers, or renders fierce animals tame, or feeds starving wolves out of the herds which he tends. . . . Often the saint's place of settlement is fixed by the appearance of animals, whether foretold beforehand, or accepted on the spot as an omen. His burial place is determined in the same way. It is clear that the ideas underlying many of these stories go back to a time when no hard and fast line was drawn between [humans] and animals,

when it seemed quite natural that the language of animals should be understood by [people] and vice versa, that an animal should have human understanding and enter into a [person's] thoughts; that covenants should be made with them. . . .

Not only hagiographers emphasized the Celtic saints' love of animals; other writers, including Bede the Venerable, described the early Celtic Christians as "really lovers of animals," and their saints "shared this quality to the full."

In the stories that follow, we will see that both saints *and animals* act as soul friends and mediators of wisdom, capable of inspiring a deeper spirituality, a new ethic of holiness for our own time. Let us turn now to those stories, and the illustrations that accompany them, allowing them to become our spiritual mentors and guides. As we reflect upon these tales, let us ask ourselves these questions:

- What can this story teach us about our own spirituality and call to service and leadership today?

- What lessons or virtues is the story affirming for our own lives?

- What is this lesson teaching us about wisdom and a spirituality that might well change our lives and our attitudes toward all of creation and the loving God who made us all? As Saint Columban said, "If you wish to know the Creator, come to know his creatures."

On our own sacred journeys through time, may we begin to see both the Celtic saints and the animals with whom we live today as true soul friends leading us into a deeper spirituality. I encourage you to recall your own experiences of loving creatures; acknowledge the gifts they have given you with their love. If you are in touch with animals today, in whatever form, take time to observe what they may be trying to teach you. You may find they provide you with messages and awareness that enrich your daily sense of beauty, giving you reasons for gratitude.

1

Patrick of Armagh

March 17 feast day

PERHAPS THE MOST WELL-KNOWN CELTIC
saint of all times is Patrick who lived from about 390 to
461. Along with Brigit and Columcille, he is considered to be
one of "the holy trinity of Celtic saints."

The patron saint of Ireland, he was, however, not born
there but possibly near the west coast of England or Wales or,
more likely, Brittany. Raised in a Christian family (his father
was a deacon and his grandfather a priest), Patrick, at the age
of fifteen, was captured by Irish pirates and taken against his
will to Ireland, where he lived for six years as a slave. There,

while tending sheep alone on a mountainside, except most likely accompanied by a dog (a great variety of dogs, from wolfhounds to greyhounds to terriers, lapdogs, and collies, were common then), he experienced a religious conversion. As he writes in an autobiography, *The Confession*, about his experience shepherding "day after day," "more and more the love of God grew strong within me." Visited by voices and dreams, he eventually escaped back to his homeland after six years, only to return to Ireland after another vivid dream in which he heard the voices of the Irish calling, "Come back, O youth, and walk among us once more."

The earliest hagiography of Patrick, by Muirchu, written some two hundred years after the saint's death, contains stories relating how Patrick changes himself and his men into deer in order to hide from a pursuing chieftain who refused to accept the new Christian faith the saint was preaching. Another deer story tells how on the hilltop near Armagh, Ireland, where a church still stands today, he comes upon a hind (a female deer) with her fawn while searching for a place to build his monastery.

Patrick's Shape-Shifting

After Patrick returned to Ireland to bring the Irish the gospel, a certain King Loegaire and his followers were angry with

Patrick, and the king determined to kill Patrick. Loegaire said to his men, "Lay hands on this fellow who is destroying us."

At this, Patrick rose and said in a clear voice, "May God arise, and God's enemies be scattered and those who hate flee from God's face." And immediately, darkness fell on them, and there was a horrible sort of upheaval and the ungodly attacked one another. There was a great earthquake that locked their chariot-axles together and drove them off violently, until in the end, only a few of them escaped half-dead to the mountain Monduirn. Only the king, his wife, two other kings, and another four followers remained alive. And they were very frightened.

The queen came to Patrick and said to him, "Sir, you are just and powerful; do not destroy the king, for the king will come and bend the knee before you, and worship your Lord." The king came, then, compelled by fear, and bowed before the saint and pretended to worship the God whom he did not want to accept.

After they had taken leave of each other, the king, going a little way off, called Saint Patrick over on some pretext, with the intention of killing him. But Patrick, aware of the king's thoughts, first blessed his companions in the name of Jesus Christ and then turned toward the king. The king counted Patrick and his men as they approached—but immediately they disappeared from the king's sight. He and his men saw only eight deer with a fawn.

King Loegaire, saddened, frightened, and humiliated, returned at dawn to Tara with the few survivors. Patrick, following Jesus' command to go forth and teach all nations and baptize them in the name of the Creator, the Son, and the Holy Spirit, set out from Tara and preached, with Christ working with him and confirming his words with powerful signs.

Patrick and His Charioteer's Horses

One night, as Patrick and his men traveled across Ireland, his charioteer realized his horses had gone astray and was grieving about this as if he had just lost close friends. He told Patrick, but as it was dark, he could not go and search for them.

Patrick was moved to kindness like a good father, and he said to the tearful charioteer, "God is always ready to help us in our difficulties, and grants us mercy in all our misfortunes. So you shall find these horses that you are crying over."

Then holding out his hand, and drawing clear his sleeve, Patrick raised his hand—and his five fingers shone out like spotlights. They lit up all the area around about them and in that light, the man was able to find his missing horses.

But it should be noted that this miracle was not known about during Patrick's lifetime because the charioteer told no one about it until after Patrick's death.

Patrick Saves a Fawn

Some time later, there was in the country a rich and respected man called Daire. Patrick asked him to give him some place for his religious observances. And the rich man said to the saint, "What place do you want?"

"I want," said Patrick, "you to give me that piece of high ground that is called Willow Ridge, and I will build a monastery there." And they both went out, Saint Patrick and Daire, to look at the wonderful offering and pleasing gift.

When they climbed up to that high ground, they found a hind with her little fawn lying on the spot where now there is the altar of the North Church in Armagh. Patrick's companions wanted to take hold of the fawn and kill it, but the saint refused and did not allow it; indeed the saint himself took the fawn, carrying it on his shoulders; and the hind followed him like a very gentle, docile ewe, till he had let the fawn go free in another wood lying to the north side of Armagh. The knowledgeable say that in that wood there are some signs remaining to this day of Patrick's miraculous power.

2

Brigit of Kildare

February 1 feast day

BRIGIT (ALSO SPELLED BRIGID) LIVED IN Ireland from about 452 to 524, governing both women and men in her double-monastery at Kildare. She seems to have had all the powers of a bishop in her community, and there are even stories of her having been ordained as such by a Bishop Mel. Considered one of the "holy trinity" of Irish saints, she has so many stories of her great compassion for both humans and animals that she is similar to the bodhisattva Quan Yin, the Buddhist goddess of mercy, who is worshipped in China, Japan, and other East Asian countries, and who is, like Brigit, seen as the protector of animals.

In Ireland, Brigit is still prayed to as the guardian of farm animals. Her *Life* was written by Cogitosus, a monk at Kildare, about a hundred years after her death. In the stories about her, she is portrayed as an exceptionally kind person to both her fellow humans, especially the poor and ill, as well as animals of every kind, all of whom seem to have responded to her love with trust and gratitude.

Brigit and the Hungry Dog

As Brigit grew into adulthood, everything to which her hand was set increased. She tended sheep, she satisfied the birds, she fed the poor.

Once when a noble guest came to her father Dubthach's house, and hospitality was naturally expected to be shown, Brigit was in the kitchen preparing the meal. As she was cooking five pieces of bacon for the guest, a hungry hound came into the kitchen. Out of pity for him, Brigit gave him a piece of bacon. The hound, however, was not satisfied with that—so Brigit gave him another piece.

She thought the guest would not notice, but he did and went to Dubthach to complain. Dubthach then asked his daughter, "Have you boiled the bacon, and do all the portions remain?"

"Count them," Brigit responded.

When her father counted them, he discovered that not one piece was missing! This was a relief to him, but he was not happy about the guest's accusation, and, as a result, the guest was not given the bacon. Instead, at Brigit's suggestion, it was given to the poor and needy, while the happy hound went away filled as well.

The Wild Fox and Brigit's Compassion

On a certain occasion, when a foolish man saw a fox walking toward the castle of the Irish king, he thought it was a wild animal. Dimwitted as he was, he was ignorant of the fact that the fox was tame, a frequent visitor to the king's court and trained in various skills. The fox was, in short, a grand and distinguished mascot of the king and his nobles. The poor fool, however, killed the fox.

At once, the man was denounced by those who had witnessed the deed. They put him in irons and dragged him before the king. When the king learned what had happened, he was enraged. He ordered the man to be killed, unless a fox, as clever as his own, were given to him in recompense. The king also ordered the man's wife, his children, and all that he had to be reduced to slavery.

When holy and venerable Brigit learned what had happened, she felt great compassion for the miserable fool and ordered her chariot to be prepared. Grieving in her innermost heart for the poor unfortunate, she rode along the road that led to the castle of the king, pouring out prayers to God as she passed over the flat plain.

There was no delay, for the Holy One heard Brigit as she continued to pray so fervently. God commanded a fox to go to her. When the fox approached the speeding chariot of holy Brigit, he leaped up lightly and landed inside. Then, nestling up under the fold of Brigit's garment, he sat tamely in the chariot with her.

As soon as Brigit arrived at the king's castle, she began to beg that the poor fool who had killed the king's fox be set free. The king was unwilling to listen to her pleas, swearing that he would not free the man unless he was recompensed with a fox as gentle and as clever as his had been.

At this point, Brigit brought forth her fox into the center of the court. The fox played before the eyes of everyone in exactly the same way as the other fox had done, acting before the king and all those gathered there with the same gestures, cleverness, and docility as the first fox had.

When the king saw this, he was satisfied and, acknowledging the resounding approval of the multitude who were in admiration of this wondrous event, he ordered the man who had earlier been charged with a crime to be released and set free. Not much later, when Saint Brigit had returned to her home, the same fox, sad and teased by the crowds, fled through the remote forests and reached his own cave unharmed.

The Wide Variety of Animals Who Listened to Brigit and Loved Her

On one occasion a wild boar, who was being hunted, came running out of the woods in terror and suddenly landed in the midst of blessed Brigit's pigs. She noted its arrival and pronounced a blessing upon it. Thereupon the boar lost its terror and settled down among the herd. See, brothers and sisters, how even brute animals and creatures were unable to resist her words and her will but served her tamely and obediently!

On another day, the blessed Brigit saw some ducks swimming on the water, occasionally taking wing. Being moved with affection for them, she commanded them to come to her. A great flock of them flew over to her on feathered wings with eager obedience to her words, showing no fear. She touched them with her hands and caressed them for a while before they returned to their place of origin.

From this and so many other stories we can easily conclude that all kinds of wild animals, flocks, and birds listened to Brigit and loved her.

3

Columcille of Iona

June 9 feast day

THE THIRD SAINT OF "THE HOLY TRINITY," Columcille, lived from 521 to 597. He was born in Donegal, Ireland and after his ordination as a priest, founded numerous monasteries in Ireland, including Derry, Durrow, and Kells. All of these had oak groves, the favorite trees of druids and druidesses, growing on their original sites. (Kildare, for example, the site of Saint Brigit's monastery, where originally an "eternal flame" was kept burning by druidesses, means "church of the oak.")

At the age of forty-two, Columcille left Ireland and moved to the island of Iona, where he founded one of the greatest monasteries in the early Celtic church, still a very popular place of pilgrimage today. A poet, scholar, and writer, his hagiography was written by his successor, Adamnan (c. 624–704), the ninth abbot of that monastery. Adamnan described Columcille's care for animals and birds, and their love for him in return.

The most famous story, perhaps, is the one of his solicitude for a tired crane, revealing that, as much as the Rule of Saint Benedict encourages every guest to be treated as another Christ, here in Columcille's monastery, evidently even animals were treated in that way!

Another, less-known story indicates that Columcille's compassion was manifest in his demand that no animals be killed or eaten at his monastery, suggesting that he was a vegetarian, if not outright vegan. (Other saints, as we will see, followed a similar diet.) Such love and compassion toward animals, it seems, was well-received, for in another story, as Columcille prepares to die, his grieving white horse, comes to tell him goodbye.

Columcille and the Tired Crane

While Columcille was living on Iona, he called one of the brothers to him and said, "Three days from now, in the morning, you must sit down and wait for a crane on the shore on the western side of this island. A stranger from the northern region of Ireland, it has been driven about by various winds. This crane will come, weary and fatigued, after the ninth hour [3 p.m.]. She will be quite exhausted. Treat that bird tenderly, and take her to some nearby house, where you can kindly and carefully nurse her and feed her for three days and three nights. When the crane is refreshed after three days of rest, and is no longer willing to stay with us, she will fly back with renewed strength to the pleasant part of Ireland from which she originally came. I entrust this bird to you with special care because she comes from our native land."

The brother obeyed Columcille, and on the third day, after the ninth hour, he watched as he had been told for the arrival of the expected guest. As soon as the crane came and alighted on the shore, the brother gently picked up the weak and hungry bird and carried her to a dwelling that was nearby, where he fed her.

On the monk's return to the monastery that evening, Columcille, without any inquiry but as if stating a fact, said to him, "God bless you, my son, for your kind attention to this foreign visitor who will not remain here for very long but will return within three days to her old home."

It happened exactly as the saint predicted, for after being nursed carefully for three days, the bird flapped her wings and gently rose to a great height, while her generous host watched.

Then, on that calm day, she made her way through the air homeward, flying straight across the sea to Ireland.

Columcille's Admonition to Do No Harm

Another time, a certain brother called Molua approached the saint while he was writing, and said, "Please bless this implement I am holding." Stretching out his holy hand, with the pen still in it, Columcille made the sign of the cross without looking up from the book he was copying.

Now when Molua had gone away with the blessed implement, Columcille said, as an afterthought, "What was that implement I blessed for our brother?"

"A knife," said Diarmait, his faithful attendant, "for slaughtering bulls and cattle."

"I trust in my God," the saint replied, "that the implement I blessed will do no harm to people or animals."

These words of Columcille came true that very hour. The owner of the knife went out beyond the enclosure of the monastery intending to kill a bullock. Three times he tried, pressing hard, but he could not pierce the skin. So the skillful monks melted down the iron knife and coated all the knives of the monastery with it. After that, none of the knives could do any harm, since the saint's blessing remained on them so strongly.

Columcille and the White Horse

As a true prophet, Columcille knew long before his death when he would die. One day during the month of May, the old man, worn out with age, went in a chariot to visit some of the brethren who were at work. When he had found them on the western side of Iona, he began to speak to them, saying, "With great yearning, during the paschal solemnities this past April, I desired to depart to Christ the Lord, and he gave me permission to do so, if I wished. But rather than have a joyous feast turned for you into mourning, I thought it better to put off for a little longer the time of my departure from the world."

The beloved monks, upon hearing this sad news, were greatly affected. Columcille tried as best he could to cheer them with words of consolation. Then, having done this, he turned his face to the east, still seated as he was in his chariot, and blessed the island with its inhabitants. From that day to the present, the venomous reptiles with the three forked tongues could do no harm to human or beast.

On Columcille's way back to the monastery, he rested halfway at a place where a cross was later erected. (It is standing to this day, fixed into a millstone, and can be observed on the roadside.) While the saint, bowed down with old age, sat there to rest a little, a white packhorse came up to him. She was the same willing servant who used to carry the milk vessels from the cowshed to the monastery.

As the horse came up to the saint, she laid her head on his bosom—inspired by God to do so, I believe, since each animal is gifted with the knowledge of things according to the will of the Creator. Somehow knowing that her master was soon about to leave her, and that she would see him no more, this white horse began to neigh plaintively. Like a human being, she shed copious tears on the saint's chest.

When Columcille's attendant saw this, he began to drive the weeping mourner away, but the saint forbade him, saying: "Let it be, Diarmait. Since the horse is so fond of me, let her shed her tears of grief on my chest. Consider this: since you are human and have a rational soul, you cannot know anything of my departure, except what I myself have just told you. But to this humble beast, devoid of reason, the Creator has evidently in some way revealed that her master is about to leave." Saying this, the saint blessed the horse.

4

Brendan of Clonfert

May 16 feast day

PROBABLY THE MOST WELL-KNOWN CELTIC saint, after the holy trinity of saints, is Brendan the Navigator whose journey, as recorded in the *Voyage of Brendan*, became one of the most popular stories of the Middle Ages. Written possibly as early as 800, it tells of Brendan's search for the Promised Land of the Saints, and it became so popular that it influenced other explorers, including Christopher Columbus, to set sail into the unknown from Europe,

The epic of Brendan's voyage is an example of that literary genre peculiar to Ireland called an *immram,* associated with the seafaring adventures of Celtic heroes. Brendan's story was probably influenced by an immram tale of a pre-Christian adventurer, the *Voyage of Bran*, and it was influential in another immram story, the *Voyage of Mael Duin*. Some of the adventures described in Brendan's story also seem to have been influenced by Homer's *Odyssey* and Virgil's *Aeneid,* which Irish monks would have known about at the time Brendan's voyage was written down. Some scholars believe his story is actually an account of his travel to Greenland, if not North America itself.

Brendan the saint, though his life is associated with fabulous legends and adventures, was a real person who lived from 486 to 578. He was born on the west coast of Ireland, founded several monasteries (the most famous that of Clonfert), and we know he did make voyages to the Scottish isles and perhaps to Wales and northwestern England as well.

The *Voyage of Brendan* is filled with stories of animals: a helpful dog, birds who guide him and his monks, and a whale who provides shelter. It also describes Brendan's decision to never eat meat. He is considered the patron saint of boatmen, mariners, travelers, elderly adventurers, and whales.

Brendan and His Monks Set Sail,
Helped by a Dog Who Guides Them

Saint Brendan and those with him got iron tools and constructed a light boat with a ribbed wooden frame, as is usual in those parts. They covered it with ox-hides tanned with the bark of oak and smeared all the joints of the hides on the outside with fat. They carried into the boat hides for the makings of two other boats, supplies for forty days, fat for preparing hides to cover the boat, and other things needed for human life. They also placed a mast in the middle of the boat and a sail and the other requirements for steering a boat.

Then Saint Brendan ordered his brothers in the name of the Creator, Son, and Holy Spirit to enter the boat. Brendan then embarked; the sail was spread, and they began to steer westward into the summer solstice. They had a favorable wind and, apart from holding the sail, had no need to navigate.

After fifteen days, the wind dropped. They set themselves to the oars until their strength failed. Brendan quickly began to comfort and advise them, saying: "Brothers, do not fear. God is our helper, sailor, and helmsperson. God guides us. Ship all the oars and the rudder. Just leave the sail spread, and God will do whatever God wants, with us and with our ship."

When they got a wind, they did not know from what direction it came or in what direction the boat was going. When forty days were up, and all the victuals had been consumed, an island appeared toward the north, rocky and high. When they had circled the island for three days, on the third day about three o'clock they found an opening where one boat might enter. Brendan stood up immediately and blessed the entry.

It was a cutting with rock of remarkable height on either side, straight up like a wall. When they had all disembarked and stood outside on land, Brendan forbade them to take any equipment out of the boat. As they were walking along the cliffs of the sea, a dog ran across the path and came to the feet of Brendan, as dogs usually come to heel to their human companions.

Brendan said to his brothers, "Has not God sent us a good messenger? Follow him."

Then Saint Brendan and his brothers followed the dog to a town. On entering the town, they caught sight of a great hall, furnished with beds and chairs, with water for washing their tired feet. After entering, Saint Brendan spoke to a man who was there, "Bring the meal that God has sent us."

This man found a table, made it ready for them, and brought each of them a loaf of marvelous whiteness, and also fish. When everything was placed on the table, Saint Brendan blessed the meal and said to his brothers, "Give praise to the God of heaven who gives food to all flesh."

Brendan and the Whale

One day as Brendan and his fellow monks were traversing the sea in search of the Promised Land, they approached an island that had no grass growing on it. There were a few pieces of driftwood on it, but no sand on its shore. Disembarking on it, the brothers spent the night outside in prayers and vigils, while Brendan remained sitting inside the boat. He knew what kind of island it was, but did not want to tell them, lest they be terrified.

When morning came, while Brendan sang the Mass in the boat, some of the brothers put a pot over a fire they had started. Suddenly, however, when the wood was burning, and the pot began to boil, the island began to heave and sway like a wave hitting a shore. The brothers rushed to the boat, crying out for protection.

Clasping their hands, Brendan drew each one of them into the boat. Once everyone was onboard, they quickly left the island and set sail. Then, before their bewildered eyes, the island itself on which they had camped moved out to sea!

"Brothers," Brendan asked, "are you surprised at what this island has done?"

They responded in unison: "Dear father, not only are we surprised, but, truly, we are terrified."

He, in response, gently told them, "My sons, don't be afraid. God revealed to me during the night in a dream the secret of this happening. Where we were was not an island, but a fish—and no ordinary fish, but a whale, the most giant fish that swims in the ocean. His name is Jasconius. Do not be afraid; he will offer us a place for shelter again." And then, smiling broadly, Brendan also advised: "Just don't light any more fires on his back!"

The Paradise of Birds and the One Who Offers Hope and Guidance

When they were sailing near another island where they had spent three days and came to the western edge of it, they saw another island almost joining it, separated only by a small channel. There was plenty of grass on it; it had groves of trees and was full of flowers. They started circling it, looking for a landing place, and as they were sailing on its southern side, they found a stream flowing into the sea. There they put the boat in to land.

As they disembarked, Saint Brendan ordered them to draw the boat with ropes up along the riverbed with all their might. The father sat in the boat. So they carried on for about a mile until they came to the source of the stream.

Brendan said, "Our Lord Jesus Christ has given us a place in which to stay during his holy Resurrection." He added, "If we had no other supplies but this spring, it would, I believe, alone be enough for food and drink."

Beside the spring stood a tree of extraordinary girth and no less height covered with white birds. The birds covered it so completely the men could scarcely see its leaves or branches. When the man of God saw this, he began to think and ponder within himself what it meant; what was the reason that such a great multitude of birds could be all collected together?

He was so tormented about this that tears poured out and flowed down upon his cheeks, and he implored God, saying, "God who knows the unknown and reveals all that is secret, you know the distress of my heart. I implore your Majesty to have pity and reveal to me, a sinner, through your great mercy your secret that I now look upon with my eyes. I rely not on what I deserve or my worth, but rather on your boundless pity."

When he said this within himself and had taken his seat again, one of the birds flew from the tree, making a noise with her wings like a handbell, and took up position on the side of the boat where Brendan was sitting. She sat on the edge of the prow and stretched her wings, as if giving a sign of joy, and looked with a peaceful mien at the holy father.

Brendan immediately concluded that God had listened to his plea. He said to the bird, "If you are God's messenger, tell me where these birds come from and why they are congregated here."

She replied immediately, " We survive the great destruction of the ancient enemy, but we were not associated with him through any sin of ours. When we were created, Lucifer's fall and that of his followers brought about our destruction also. But our God is just and true. Divine Mercy sent us here, where we endure no suffering. Here we can see God's presence. But God has separated us from sharing the lot of the others who were faithful. We wander through various regions of the air and the firmament and the Earth, just like the other spirits that travel on their missions. But on holy days and Sundays, we are given bodies such as you now see so that we may stay here and praise our Creator. You and your brothers have now spent one year on your journey. Six still remain. Where you celebrated Easter today, there you will celebrate it every year. Afterward, you will find what you cherish in your heart, that is, the Promised Land of the Saints."

After she said this, the bird lifted herself off the prow and flew to the other birds.

Brendan, Vegetarian or Vegan

The venerable father and his companions sailed out into the ocean, and their boat was carried along for another forty days. One day, there appeared to them a beast of immense size following them at a distance. He spouted foam from his nostrils and plowed through the waves at a great speed, as if he were about to devour them.

Saint Brendan comforted his companions, saying, "Do not be afraid. You have little faith. God, who always defends us, though, will deliver us from the mouth of this beast and from other dangers."

As the beast came near them, he caused waves of extraordinary height to go before him right up to the boat, so that the brothers were more and more afraid. The venerable elder raised his hands to heaven and said, "Lord, deliver your servants, as you delivered David from the hand of Goliath, the giant. Lord, deliver us, as you delivered Jonas from the belly of the whale."

After these pleas asking for deliverance, the brothers saw a mighty monster pass near them from the west, going to encounter the beast. This monster immediately attacked the other creature, emitting fire from his mouth. The wretched beast that had pursued the servants of Christ was cut into three pieces before their eyes. The other monster returned to where he had come from.

The next day, they saw at a distance a very large island full of trees. After they drew near its shore and disembarked from the boat, they saw the end portion of the beast that had been slain. Brendan said, "See what wished to devour you, you shall now devour! Take your provisions from that beast, enough for three months. For tonight its flesh will be devoured by other beasts."

The brothers set out to the place to do so. They brought back as much as they could carry. The venerable father said to them, "Keep it and preserve it carefully with salt. You will have need of it. For God will make the weather fine today, tomorrow, and after-morrow. The swell of the sea and the waves will fall. Then we will leave this place."

When these days were over, Saint Brendan ordered his brothers to load the boat, fill the containers, and other vessels and collect plants and roots for his own use. For Brendan, ever since the time of his ordination to the priesthood, had tasted nothing in which the spirit of life drew support from flesh.

When all was loaded into the boat, they raised the sail and set off in a northerly direction, toward the Promised Land of the Saints.

5

Ciaran of Saighir

March 5 feast day

CIARAN IS CONSIDERED THE FIRST SAINT TO have been born in Ireland; he was born about 446 and died about 530. One of Saint Patrick's earliest disciples, he is said to have received his early education in Tours in Gaul and also in Rome, where he was ordained. He then went to live as a hermit near Saighir, told to do so by Patrick himself.

There, near the Slieve Bloom Mountains, in a solitary forest on the bank of a small stream, Ciaran built a hut of wattles and twigs, smeared with mud, and thatched with leaves and grass. A vegetarian, he ate only a little barley bread and herbs, and his drink was water from the well. Although many disciples joined him, attracted by his holiness, his first monks, as we discover in the stories about him, were wild animals from the forest.

Ciaran's First Miracle: Saving a Small Bird

The most blessed Ciaran, the first begotten of the saints of Ireland, belonged to the west border of Leinster, which is called Ossory. At the time of his birth, none of the folk of Ireland were Christian. His father was called Luaigne, his mother Liadain. Ciaran was brought up on Cape Clear Island.

Truly God chose him from his mother's womb, for when the name of Christ was not yet heard in Ireland, the strength of the Christian faith began to grow in him. His parents wondered at this, and all who saw him remarked on the soberness of his mind, the gentleness of his nature, the sweetness of his words, his timely fasting, his wise counsels, and many other qualities that belong to holy people.

One day on this same Cape Clear Island, the first of Saint Ciaran's miracles occurred when he was still a lad. A hawk swept down from the sky upon a small bird sitting on its nest, caught it before Ciaran's eyes, and carried it off in its talons into the air. The boy saw it and was in deep grief over it.

He prayed for the poor captive—and immediately, the eagle flew down with its prey, and laid the small bird, mangled and half-dead, on the ground before Ciaran. Under the pitying gaze of the lad, the creature by God's grace was made whole, to Ciaran's heart's desire. It fluttered away and sat brooding on its nest, happy and unhurt.

Ciaran's First Monks:
Brothers Fox, Badger, Wolf, and Deer

For thirty years, Ciaran lived in Ireland, in holiness and integrity of body and soul, without baptism, for the Irish had not been converted to Christianity. Nevertheless, by the inspiration of the Holy Spirit, Ciaran lived devoutly and perfectly in his ways.

Hearing a report of the Christian faith in the city of Rome, he left Ireland and set out for Rome. On reaching it, he was baptized and taught the Christian faith. There he remained for twenty years, reading the Holy Scriptures, and collecting books on their meaning. Seeing the wisdom, devotion, and faith of Ciaran, the Roman people ordained him bishop, and then sent him back to his own land.

On the road back through Italy, Ciaran met Saint Patrick, and the two saints, in meeting face to face, were extremely happy. Patrick said to Ciaran, "Go to Ireland before me; and make your way to a well in the heart of Ireland, on the border between the men of the North and the men of the South. The well is called Fuaran, the little cold well, and there found your monastery, for in that place shall your glory and your resurrection be."

The two servants of God kissed and blessed each other. Saint Ciaran went on his way toward Ireland, but the blessed Patrick stayed behind for a time in Italy.

Now when Ciaran arrived in Ireland, God guided him to the well of Fuaran. He began to live as a hermit there, for the place was a vast solitude and thick with forest. He built himself a poor cell that became the beginning of a monastery. Thereafter, by God's gift and through the grace of Ciaran, a city grew up.

But when Saint Ciaran had first come to that place, he sat himself down under a tree. In the tree's shadow, he found a fierce boar. The boar, seeing for the first time the face of a human, fled in terror. But then, made tame by God, he came back to Ciaran volunteering to be his servant.

That boar was Saint Ciaran's first disciple in that place, the first brother to join him. The boar, as the man of God watched, began with great vigor to tear down twigs and grass with his teeth to build Ciaran a little hut.

Later, other animals came from their dens in the wilds to Saint Ciaran, a fox, a badger, a wolf, and a deer, and they stayed

with him, tame and gentle. They obeyed the saint's words in all
things, as if they had been his monks.

The Wily Fox and the Assertive Badger

One day the Fox, who was shrewder and wilier than the other
animals, stole Abbot Ciaran's shoes, and abandoning his vow
of poverty, Fox carried them off to his ancient dwelling in the
forest, where he intended to chew them. Knowing this, Ciaran
sent another monk, namely the Badger, into the forest after the
Fox, to bring back his brother to the monastery.

So the Badger, being well acquainted with the woods,
at once set out in obedience to his abbot's orders and made
his way to the den of Brother Fox. There, finding him about to
gnaw his master's slippers, he bit his ears and his tail, cropped
his fur, and forced him to return with him to the monastery,
there to do penance for his theft. The Fox, driven by necessity,
and the Badger with him carrying the shoes (none the worse),
came to Ciaran in his cell.

The saint said to the Fox, "Why, brother, did you do
this evil deed, which good monks would not do? Behold, our
water is sweet and free to us, and food is here for us all alike to
share. And if you had a longing, as is your nature, to eat flesh,
Almighty God would have made it for you from the roots of
these trees, if we had asked."

The Fox begged the saint's forgiveness and did penance fasting, not eating until he was given the saint's okay. And thereafter he lived sociably with the others.

In the end, Ciaran's disciples and many others sought him out from all parts of Ireland, and it was the beginning of a famous monastery. The animals, however, continued to live there as well for the rest of their lives, tame and loyal, for the saint was happy to see them as friends and fellow monks.

6

Colman of Kilmacduagh

October 29 feast day

THERE ARE MORE THAN FIFTY RECOGNIZED saints with the name of Colman in Ireland, but the one who is associated with the wonderful story of his animal friends was Colman mac Duagh, who was born in Kiltartan, now County Galway, and lived from about 560 to 632. He was the son of Queen Rhinagh and her husband, the chieftain named Duac, and thus, in Irish, Colman was known as mac Duach.

Educated at Saint Enda's monastery on Inishmore, the largest of the Aran Islands, he lived as a hermit there, praying and fasting constantly. Seeking greater solitude, when he was about thirty, he moved to the Burren in County Claire, accompanied by a servant, where he lived in a cave. Some twenty years later, with his relative, an Irish king, he founded the monastery of Kilmacduagh ("the church of the son of Duac"), where he was abbot for years. The ruins of this monastery, consisting of seven churches and a large, leaning round tower, are located near the town of Gort in County Galway, a holy site visited by numerous pilgrims today. His crozier can now be seen in the National Museum in Dublin.

Colman's Friends: The Rooster, the Mouse, and the Fly

Now, the Holy Spirit had endowed Colman with many virtues. He was a great lover of poverty, and he kept no earthly possessions, nor gifts, nor any property of his own—unless you could call three small creatures "property." For Colman did have three animal companions: a rooster, a mouse, and a fly, which he considered to be friends of his.

Each animal served him out of their love for him. Like an alarm clock, the rooster awakened him at a certain time of night with its crowing so that he might not miss the communal prayers at that hour. The service of the other two creatures was even more remarkable. The mouse would not allow the man of God to sleep nor lie at peace beyond the fixed hour that Colman had fixed for himself in his holy vows. When his body and his tired limbs were worn out with vigil and prayer and his other austerities, when his body craved sleep and rest beyond what he had vowed, the mouse—sometimes gnawing at his clothes, sometimes nibbling at his ear—would drag him from all quiet. Colman was grateful for this service, for the mouse helped him maintain his own self-respect so that his vows were kept. Scarcely less remarkable was the service of the fly. For when the man of God had leisure to read his holy books, the fly would trot up and down the lines, acting as a living reading aid. If someone called Colman, or he had to do some monastic task, he would instruct the fly to sit on the line at which he had had stopped reading and keep his place until he could return to finish. The fly always would happily do so for his friend.

Marvelous were these small creatures, contributing to Colman's well-being. Truly they were manifestations of God's grace in his life and of Christ's gift to the saints. For this, Colman was exceptionally grateful to the God who created all of them, and to his friends, the rooster, the mouse, and the fly, for their services that made his daily life so blessed.

7

Columban of Luxeuil

November 23 feast day

COLUMBAN IS CONSIDERED THE GREATEST of Ireland's many missionaries to the European continent in the early Middle Ages. In more recent times, he has been described, because of his knowledge of literature, composition of poetry, and his exquisite writing, as "Ireland's first man of letters," and, because of his prescient sense of European unity, as "Ireland's first European" and "a father of Christian Europe." He was born in Leinster, Ireland, about 543, probably to a noble family who was able to provide him with a good classical education before he became a monk.

When Columban joined the seaside monastery at Bangor on the Irish coast, Saint Comgall became his mentor. There, Columban was educated, ordained, and lived for many years.

In 590, at midlife, Columban, accompanied by twelve companions, including Saint Gall, left for Brittany and Gaul to spread the gospel. When he arrived in Gaul, he built a monastery at Annegray. As more followers joined him, he founded another at Luxeuil, and still another near some springs at Fontes (now called Fontaine).

Columban and Gall eventually moved on to Switzerland, where Gall remained, while the older man settled near Bobbio, Italy, dying in 615. His beautiful white marble tomb can still be seen there. Saint Francis of Assisi was one of the more famous pilgrims who visited it, and many of the Nature and animal stories later associated with Francis were originally found in Columban's hagiography, written by Jonas, a monk of Bobbio. These stories show how much Columban loved and respected animals, and they, in turn, him.

Columban's Search for Solitude and His Encounters with Bears

When Columban arrived in Gaul, he and his followers settled in an isolated place, called from ancient times Anagrates (Annegray), despite the loneliness, wilderness, and rocks. Then crowds of people and throngs of the infirm, seeking aid in all their sicknesses, began to crowd about Columban, asking him to restore their health. Unable to ignore their pleas, he healed the infirmities of all who came to him through his prayers and by relying upon the help of God.

Later, Columban withdrew from his cell, desiring to go deeper into solitude. He entered the wilderness by a longer road, and after going about seven miles, he found an immense cliff with steep sides and rocky paths. Perceiving a hollow in the rock, he entered a cave and began to explore its hidden recesses, only to discover that it was the home of a bear—and that the bear herself was there! Columban ordered the beast to leave and not return to that place. Mercifully, the bear left immediately, nor did she return.

It became Columban's custom to separate himself from the company of others and to dwell in solitary places so that when the feasts of the Lord or saints' days came, he might, with his mind wholly free from disquieting cares, devote himself to prayer. One time, Columban, a lover of solitude, happened to be walking through a dense forest of fruit trees and found a bear about to devour the body of a stag that wolves had killed.

The man of God approached the bear, who was licking up the stag's blood, but before she had eaten any of the stag's flesh, Columban ordered her not to injure the hide, which the saint needed for shoes. Then the beast, contrary to her nature, put aside her ferocity, became gentle, and without a murmur, left the stag. Columban returned to the brethren and told them of his encounter; they went to the forest and stripped the hide from the body of the stag.

The Friendly Wolves

Another time, while the saint was walking in the dark woods, a book on his shoulder, arguing with himself about Holy Scripture, the question came suddenly to his mind whether he would rather choose to suffer the outrage of humans—or the savagery of beasts. His thought drove him hard, and as he walked, he would often cross himself and pray. Finally, he said to himself that it was better to suffer the ferocity of wild beasts, which was no sin of theirs, than the cruelty of humans, to the loss of their own souls.

As he turned this over in his mind, he saw twelve wolves coming toward him. They stood around him on the right and on the left, himself in the middle of them. He stood motionless, saying, "God, look to my help. Lord, make haste to help me."

They came nearer, and their muzzles touched his clothes! While he stood quietly, unshaken, they turned, left him there, and went back to roaming through the woods.

Columban's Peaceable Kingdom

Marvel not that bird and beast should obey the command of the man of God. A servant and disciple of Columban saw evidence of his intimacy with animals. This servant, by the name of Chamnoald who later became a bishop at Lyons, used to say that he often saw Columban, as he was walking in the forest, call to him the creatures of the wild, birds and beasts. The animals would come at once, and he would stroke them with his hand and caress them; and the wild things and the birds would leap and skip about him for sheer happiness, jumping up on him as puppies jump on their masters. Even that small wild creature, the squirrel, would come at his call from the high treetops, and the saint would take it in his hand and set it on his shoulder, and it would be running and out of the folds of the hood of his habit. And this the bishop said he had often seen.

8

Cuthbert of Lindisfarne

March 20 feast day

SAINT CUTHBERT IS NORTHERN ENGLAND'S most popular saint. His *Life* was written by the great storyteller Bede the Venerable, whose grave is not far from Cuthbert's in Durham Cathedral. Cuthbert was a monk and bishop of Lindisfarne (Holy Island, as it is called), off the northeast coast of England. Both Durham and Lindisfarne are still very popular destinations for thousands of pilgrims each year.

Little is known about Cuthbert's early life, but he was probably born about 634 into an Anglo-Saxon family in southern Scotland. Despite his Saxon origins, he was very much a Celt by temperament and deeply influenced by Celtic spirituality. In 651, he joined the monastery at Melrose, on the Scottish border, which had been founded by Aidan (d. 651), an Irish monk from Columcille's monastery at Iona.

Thus began a long life of intense pastoral involvement. Cuthbert served as a guestmaster at Ripon and a prior at Lindisfarne, before moving to Inner Farne Island, not far from Lindisfarne, where he attempted to live as a solitaire. Unfortunately for Cuthbert, crowds of people sought him out for spiritual guidance. In 684, against his own wishes, he was elected a bishop, but he only agreed to accept the office after the king himself sailed to Inner Farne and begged him to do so.

The following year, Cuthbert was consecrated Bishop of Lindisfarne, and once again, he assumed a very active ministry. In 687, however, he resigned as bishop and returned to his beloved Inner Farne, where he died. His was a life, it seems, torn between his love of people and his passion for solitude. Like Patrick and Brigit too, Cuthbert shepherded sheep as a youth, and a number of Bede's stories about him reflect his love of animals and their love for him. Islands located near Inner Farne are the home today of numerous seals that bark to each other and to the passing boats of pilgrims seeking to visit the holy place.

Cuthbert's Fasting and
His Sharing Food with His Comrade

While Cuthbert was considering entering a monastery and was traveling alone, he came at the third hour of the day (9:00 a.m.) into a village he happened upon by chance. He entered the house of a certain religious housewife, wishing to rest there a little and intending to ask for food for the horse on which he was riding, rather than for himself; for it was the beginning of the winter season, and grass was scarce.

The woman received him kindly and begged him to allow her to prepare him a morning meal to refresh him. The man of God refused saying, "I cannot eat yet because it is a fast day." For it was Friday, a day on which most of the faithful are accustomed to protract their fast until the ninth hour (3 p.m.) out of reverence for the passion of the Lord.

The woman, being given to hospitality, persisted, saying, "Look, you will find no village and no human habitation on the road you are taking; and you have a long journey before you, which you cannot finish before sunset. So I pray you to accept food before you set out."

But, though she urged him, Cuthbert's commitment to fasting overcame the urgency of her entreaty, and he set out once more and fasted the whole day until evening. When evening was at hand, he discovered he could not finish the journey, and there were no lodgings in the area. He noticed, however, some shepherds' huts close by; they had been roughly built during the summertime and were now lying open and deserted.

He entered one, fastened his horse to the wall, collected a bundle of straw the wind had removed from the roof, and gave it to the horse to eat. He himself began to pray, when suddenly, in the midst of his psalm-singing, he saw the horse lift up her head, seize the thatching of the house with her mouth, and drag it down. Amid the straw falling from the roof, Cuthbert saw a folded cloth fall as well. Wishing to discover what it was, he drew near—when his prayer was finished—and found, wrapped in the cloth, half a loaf of bread, still warm, and some meat, sufficient for one meal for himself.

Then Cuthbert uttered praises, thanking God "who has deigned to provide a supper for me . . . and also for my comrade." So he divided the piece of bread he had found and gave half of it to the horse, and the rest he kept for his own food.

From that day on, he became readier than ever to fast, because he understood clearly that his food had been provided for him in a solitary place, by the gift of the One who once for many days fed the prophet Elijah in the desert with the food brought through the ministrations of birds. When there is no human to minister to God's people, the Divine uses animals to do the job.

The Ministry of His Good Friend the Eagle

Now on a certain day, Cuthbert had left the monastery to preach as he so often did, accompanied by only a boy. By afternoon, they were already tired from the long journey they had been on, and a good distance remained before they would reach the village for which they were headed.

The saint said to the boy, in order to test him, "Come, tell me, comrade, where do you intend to refresh yourself today? Or have you any resource on the way to whom you can turn?"

The boy answered, "I have long been silently pondering that matter in my heart; for we have brought with us no provisions for the journey, nor do we have anyone we know on the way who will receive us hospitably. And a great part of the journey remains which we cannot complete without suffering—if we continue our fasting."

Then the man of God replied, "Learn, my dear son, always to have faith and trust in the Lord, for the person who serves God faithfully never perishes of hunger." Looking up, he saw an eagle flying above them. "Do you see that eagle flying far off?" he asked the boy. "It is possible for God to refresh us today with that eagle's assistance."

With these words, they went on their way along a river, when suddenly they saw the eagle settling on the bank. The man of God asked, "Do you see where our friend, as I foretold, is settling? Run, I beg you, and see what food she has brought us from the Lord, and bring it quickly here."

The boy ran up and brought back a large fish the eagle had just taken from the river.

But the man of God asked, "What have you done, my son? Why have you not given our handmaiden *her* share? Cut the fish quickly in half and take her the share she deserves for ministering to us."

The boy did as he was told and carried the rest with him. When the time for eating arrived, they stopped at the next village, where they ate the fish and refreshed themselves, as well as those into whose house they entered. Then Cuthbert preached the word of God to them and praised God, for "blessed is the person whose hope is in the name of the Lord and who has not looked after vanity nor idle folly." And so they resumed their journey, setting out to reach those whom they hoped to teach about the good news of Jesus.

How Otters Warmed Saint Cuthbert's Feet

Inside the monastery, Cuthbert performed more and more signs and wonders, and his reputation increased. A certain nun called Aebbe—who was in charge of the priory at Coldingham, where she was honored for both her piety and her nobility, for she was King Oswy's sister—sent a message to Cuthbert, asking if he would come and exhort the community.

The holy man came and stayed a few days, showing them the way of salvation in deed and in word. While he was there, he continued his custom of rising in the dead of night, while everyone else was sleeping, and going outside to pray, returning just in time for morning prayers.

One night, a monk watched him sneak out, and then the monk secretly followed Cuthbert to see where he was going and what he was about. The monk watched as Cuthbert went down to the beach below the monastery; then he waded out into the sea until he was up to his neck in deep water. Waves splashed around him as he kept his vigil throughout the dark hours of the night.

At daybreak, Cuthbert came out of the water. Shivering in the cold, he knelt on the sand and prayed. Suddenly, two otters jumped out of the sea and curled around his ankles. They warmed his feet with their breath and even tried to dry him with their fur. When they had finished, they received his blessing and slipped back to their watery home.

Cuthbert returned to the monastery and was back in choir with the rest of the monks at the proper time.

9

David of Wales

March 1 feast day

SAINT DAVID (OR DEWI SANT AS THE WELSH call him) is the patron saint of Wales, and also, due to more recent recognition of his lifestyle and diet, the patron saint of vegans and vegetarians. He was born about 520, the son of Sanctus, a Welsh king, and Non, one of the great female saints of early Celtic Christianity. He founded numerous monasteries, including that called Cell Muine in the southwestern corner of Wales, where the great Cathedral of Saint David's now stands.

David appears in numerous Celtic hagiographies as a soul friend and mentor of many saints, including Maedoc of Ferns, protector of wolves, and Modomnoc, patron saint of bees and beekeepers. Other famous Irish monastic founders who visited David in his monastery were Finnian of Clonard, Senan of Scattery Island, Findbarr of Cork, and Brendan of Clonfert. He was nicknamed "the Waterman," probably because of the strict monastic rule he followed, which included abstinence from alcohol and the drinking of water only. (He also, like Cuthbert, followed the practice of praying while immersed in the sea up to his neck.)

David and his fellow monks also maintained a diet of bread and vegetables, with just a sprinkling of salt, so as not to inflict unnecessary suffering upon any creature by taking its life for food. This respect for animals was also manifest in the brothers' preference to do hard manual labor themselves rather than using cattle or oxen to help them plow the fields.

At the time of his death (in 589 or 601; historians disagree), his last words to his monks and townspeople were, "Be joyful brothers and sisters. Keep your faith, and do the little things that you have seen and learned from me."

Prophecy of David's Greatness
Through a Stag, Fish, and Hive of Bees

Although the Holy One loves and knows us all since before the creation of the world, there are some whom God makes especially known beforehand by many signs and revelations. That saint who was named David in his baptism but "Dewi" by the common people was not only foretold by authentic prophecies of angels thirty years before his birth (first to his father and then to Saint Patrick), but David was also proclaimed as one who would be enriched with mystic gifts and endowments.

On a certain occasion, his father, Sanctus by name and merits and in full enjoyment of royal power over the people of Ceredigion, heard in a dream the voice of an angel, saying, "Tomorrow you will awake and go hunting. You will kill a stag near the river, and in that place, you will find three gifts, namely, the stag which you will pursue, a fish, and a hive of bees. Now, of these three, you will set aside the honeycomb and a portion of the fish and of the stag. These you will send to Maucannus's monastery, there to be preserved for a son who will be born of you."

These three gifts foreshadowed David's life. The honeycomb declared his wisdom, for just as the honey lies embedded in the wax, so he perceived the spiritual meaning within the physical world. The fish proclaimed his abstinence, for, as the fish lives by water, so David rejected wine, fermented liquor, and everything intoxicating, living a blessed life for God on bread and water only; thus he was called "David who lives on water." The stag signified power over the ancient enemy. For as the stag, after feeding on the snakes it has destroyed, longs for a spring of water, so David selected his own well of life with a ceaseless flow of tears.

David Founds Monasteries Whose Monks Worked with Feet and Hand

David founded twelve monasteries in all. First, he reached Glastonbury in England and built a church. Next, he went to Bath, where he changed the foul water to healthy by blessing it, endowing it with a continuous heat that made it suitable for the bathing of bodies.

One day, David's three most faithful disciples came to him, accompanied by a group of their fellow disciples. One in mind and heart, they went to a place previously foretold by an angel, where, in the name of God, they lit a fire. There at Menevia, on the site the angel had previously shown them, the community in the Lord's name built a noble monastery.

When this was all completed, such an asceticism did the holy father decree that every monk toiled at daily labor and spent his life working with his hands for the community. Knowing that idle rest was the source and the mother of vices, David bowed down the shoulders of the monks with pious labors, for those who give into idleness develop a spirit of instability and apathy with restless lustful urges.

David's monks eagerly worked with feet and hands. They placed the yoke upon their shoulders, dug the earth unweariedly with mattocks and spades, and carried in their holy hands hoes and saws for cutting. With their own efforts, they provided for all the necessities of the community. Possessions they scorned, the gifts of the wicked they rejected, and riches they abhorred. They brought in no oxen to help themselves. The work completed, no complaint was heard. When labor in the field was finished, they returned to the monastery's cloisters and spent the remainder of the day reading, writing, or praying.

A Simple Vegetarian Diet in the Monastery

Everyone restored and refreshed his weary limbs by partaking of supper, but not to excess, for too much, though it be of bread alone, engenders self-indulgence. At meal, all took supper according to the varying conditions of their bodies or age. They did not serve courses of different flavors nor richer kinds of food: their food was, in fact, bread and herbs seasoned with salt, while they quenched a burning thirst with a temperate kind of drink. Meanwhile, for either the sick, those advanced in age, or those wearied by a long journey, they provided some dishes of tastier food, since it was not proper to apportion to all in equal measure. When thanks had been given to God, they went to the church, and there they gave themselves up to prayer. Then they composed their limbs for sleep. In all things, they imitated the monks of the Egyptian desert and lived a life like theirs.

10

Gall of Saint Gallen

October 16 feast day

THE TWO GREAT IRISH MISSIONARIES, Columban and Gall traveled from Ireland to the European continent, bringing the gospel message. Gall was probably born about 560 and was placed at an early age in the monastery in Bangor, where he became Columban's pupil. Ordained a priest at the age of thirty, he set out with Columban for the Continent in 590.

After Columban had founded three monasteries in France, the two friends traveled on to Germany and then to the shores of Lake Zurich in Switzerland. There they settled down for two years. Gall was assigned important pastoral and liturgical responsibilities, as well as the duty of catching fish in the nearby lake for their suppers.

Although he was a scholar and an excellent preacher, Gall is more often associated with his fondness of solitude and fishing. This is perhaps why he is often portrayed in paintings and statues holding a fisherman's net. He also is associated in art with a bear, which is generally represented standing on its hind legs and carrying a log.

Gall and Columban parted ways when the older man decided to continue his missionary travels into Italy. While Columban moved on to Bobbio, Gall built a hermitage that was the origin of the beautiful city Saint Gallen.

After Gall's death (about 630), a Benedictine monastery was built which became one of the most famous centers of scholarship in Europe for over a thousand years. It also soon became a favorite place of pilgrimage because it contained Gall's relics. As the following stories show, Saint Gall was helped by both a friendly bear and otters who came to his rescue in times of need.

Gall, the Fisherman, and the Friendly Bear

Now Hiltibod, the deacon of the priest Willimar, was thoroughly familiar with every nook and cranny of the wilderness, for he loved to roam through it. Through daily habit, he had come to know its inmost recesses. Gall, increasingly admitting Hiltibod into his friendship, asked him if he had ever found in the wilderness any spot abounding in pure, wholesome water. "For," he told Hiltibod, "I am filled with a burning desire to pass the days I have left on this earth in some retreat."

The deacon replied, "This wilderness, my father, has many waters flowing through it, but it is a wild and fearsome place, full of high mountains with narrow winding glens and haunted by savage beasts. Besides stags and such harmless animals, it breeds countless bears and boars and wolves who are exceedingly fierce. Were I to lead you there, I fear they would devour you."

"The apostle Paul," rejoined the holy man, "has said, 'If God be for us, who can be against us?' and again, 'We know that all things work together for good to them that love God.' The One who delivered Daniel from the lions' den can also save me from the clutches of wild beasts."

Then the deacon answered Gall, "Put some food into your satchel and the smallest of your fishing nets. Tomorrow, I will lead you into the wilderness. If you find a spot that suits you, give thanks to God. For God who has brought you from a far country will send an angel with us, even as God gave a companion to Tobias, and will show us some spot suited to our desires."

The saint thus remained fasting for the rest of that day and spent the night in prayer until the dawn. Then the athlete of God, after praying and taking with him the things his guide had told him, set out on his way, with the deacon leading the way. They journeyed throughout the day until they came to the stream called Steinaha and followed its course until they reached the cliff from which descends the rushing water that forms a fine pool below.

Here, they saw a quantity of fish and, throwing their nets into the water, they caught some. Then they kindled a fire, boiled the fish, and laid out the bread they had brought with them. Gall retired a short distance to pray.

As he was walking through the tangled underbrush, his foot caught on something, and he fell to the ground. The deacon ran to him, but the man of God, filled with the spirit of prophecy, said, "Let me be. This shall be my resting place forever. Here will I dwell, for God has chosen it." And, after praying, Gall rose to his feet, took a hazel twig, formed it into a cross, and fixed it in the ground.

While he was thus engaged, a bear came down from the mountains and began stealthily to pick up the crumbs and morsels the two men had dropped. When Gall saw this, he said to the beast, "In the name of the Lord, I command you to take up a log and throw it on the fire." The bear turned at his command, brought some logs, and threw them into the fire.

The deacon, in the meantime, pretending to be asleep, observed all of this. At last, he rose and threw himself at the saint's feet, saying, "Now I know truly that the Lord is with you, since even the beasts of the wilderness serve you."

But the saint answered him, "Take heed that you tell no one of this until you see the glory of God."

Gall and the Helpful Otters

Some time later, Euastasius, abbot of the monastery of Luxeuil in Gaul, who had been appointed by Columban of happy memory, passed from the exile of this life to the homeland on high. The monks gathered and decided to recall Gall as abbot. They sent six of their number who had originally come from Ireland to bear him a letter setting forth their wishes.

When they arrived at Gall's hermitage and presented the letter to him, he said to them, "My brothers, I left my kinsfolk and acquaintances and sought out the distant recesses of the wilderness so that I might have more leisure and freedom to serve the Lord. I have also refused the rank of bishop when it was offered to me, as well as the riches of the world. How, after giving up so much and embracing poverty, shall I again be entangled in the affairs of this life, uplifted by its honors and weighed down by its burdens? Far be it for me that having put my hand to the plough I should now look back on what I have left. You yourselves know that when I was among you, I always tried to be humble and obedient. Do you now try to encourage me to a position so exalted? No, make your plans anew, and turn elsewhere, for the Lord will not allow me to change the work I have now embraced."

Then he called one of his monks and asked what they were to have for their next meal. On hearing that there was only a small measure of flour for them all, he ordered them to make it into loaves and gather some vegetables. Then he took his net and, accompanied by one of his disciples and the brethren who had just arrived, he went to the pool in the stream, saying, "Let us see whether the merciful Lord will grant us some little fishes for our needs."

On reaching the pool in which the waters of the stream were collected, they saw a big fish swimming in it, chased by two otters. The brothers threw in their net, caught the fish, and brought it to land. The otters meanwhile plunged into the depths and drove such a multitude of fish into the net that it burst in several places. As soon as they had landed their catch, the saint said to the brethren, "It is because of your coming today that the Lord has given us this wondrous sign of bounty."

As they returned to the monastery, they encountered a man who brought the saint as proof of his devotion two skins full of wine and three bushels of floor. These gifts were thankfully received, and all partook of the abundance of food. Gall kept his visitors for some days and then dismissed them with the kiss of peace. Armed with his blessing, they returned home.

11

Gobnait of Ballyvourney

February 11 feast day

ESCRIBED IN AN EARLY MEDIEVAL TEXT AS "in God's love she was a complete treasure," Gobnait was born in Ireland in the sixth century. The name Gobnait is Irish for Abigail, meaning bringer of joy, but as the patron saint of beekeepers (along with Saints Ambrose and Modomnoc), her name has often been anglicized as Deborah, meaning honeybee. Most likely she was born in north Clare and may have been a descendant of Conaire the Great, king of Ireland. Her first hermitage was near the Cliffs of Moher, before she moved to

Inis Oirr, the smallest of the Aran Islands. She later journeyed to Ballyvourney (which means "town of the beloved"), where she became abbess of a monastery. She stayed there for the rest of her life.

There are many stories of Gobnait, especially regarding her beekeeping. Renowned for her care of the sick, she used her own honey as medicine to cure illnesses. Many accounts tell of how she prevented invaders from carrying off her cattle by turning a beehive into a bronze helmet and the bees themselves into soldiers. Another version of the same story tells how she let loose the bees from her hives and they attacked invaders who sought to harm Gobnait's community.

This latter legend inspired the Harry Clarke stained-glass window in the Honan Chapel at University College Cork. This window shows the saint dressed in royal blue robes with elaborate designs in turquoise, with a silver cloak and a veil. Her face is surrounded by bees, and at her feet is a honeycomb, while the bees are depicted chasing the thieves who threaten to rob her monastery. The window also portrays Gobnait's long, pointed nose, for, according to Saint Óengus, she was "a sharp-beaked nun."

Gobnait is a very popular saint today in Ireland, with many pilgrims visiting Ballyvourney in County Cork. Other main centers of devotion to her are the Aran Islands and Dun Chaoin in West Kerry.

The following story tells of how she found what was called her "place of resurrection," the place many Celtic saints were in search of where they would die and await the resurrection of their bodies. Deer were the guides who confirmed she had found the right place (and ancient Celtic lore connects deer with the soul).

Celtic lore also believed the soul left the body as a bee or a butterfly, and thus bees were held in high esteem. It is not surprising then that Gobnait added beekeeping to her life's work, developing a lifelong affinity with them.

Gobnait and the White Deer

Born in County Clare, Gobnait fled to the island of Inisheer in the Aran Islands, escaping from her father (who was said to be a pirate). An angel had appeared to her and told her not to return to her father's ship but rather to journey inland to a place where she would find nine white deer grazing, marking the place of her resurrection.

So Gobnait traveled south in search of this place, traversing the Boggeragh Mountains, stopping near Macroon, where she saw three white deer. Since this was not the prophesied number she was looking for, she continued on to Killeen. There she saw six deer, but again, this did not fulfill the angel's words, so she went further southward. Then, across the Sullane

River and up a wooded hill, she saw them: nine white deer grazing, as the angel had said. Here, in this spot called Gort na Tiobratan, she built for herself a simple cell and prayed in gratitude to God who had led her to her place of resurrection.

Young girls came to her, seeking to join her and create a community. They herded sheep and cows, made butter and bread, and kept a hive of bees. Along with the honey, they ate vegetables and wild berries, and each evening they shared their main meal. This little community was part of the larger, surrounding community at Ballyvourney to which Gobnait and her nuns ministered, especially to the sick or those in need. Loved by many, this is where she died and was buried to await her resurrection.

12

Godric of Finchale

May 21 feast day

G ODRIC WAS AN ENGLISH HERMIT, MER-
chant, and popular medieval saint who lived from
1065 to 1170. He was born in Walpole in Norfolk and died in
Finchale in County Durham. Several hagiographies are extant,
the most important one written by a contemporary of his: a
monk named Reginald of Durham.

Godric was said to have been born into a poor family,
"slender in rank and wealth, but abundant in righteousness and
virtue." First a peddler, then a sailor, he may even have been the

captain and owner of a ship. After years at sea, Godric went to the island of Lindisfarne, the "holy isle" off the coast of England where Saint Cuthbert had lived. There he encountered Cuthbert.

This was not a physical encounter, since Cuthbert had been long dead and interred at Durham Cathedral, but a spiritual meeting with the saint that changed Godric's life. He was so impressed with the saint that he fell to his knees and begged God for the grace to be able to be like Cuthbert.

Godric began then to devote his life to service to God. After many pilgrimages, including one to Santiago de Compostella, he returned to England and lived with an elderly hermit named Aelric for two years. When Aelric died, Godric made one last pilgrimage to Jerusalem and then returned home, where he convinced the bishop of Durham to grant him a place to live as a hermit at Finchale, by the River Wear.

A vision of Saint Cuthbert led him to the site of his hermitage, and there he lived for the final sixty years of his life. As time passed, his reputation for holiness and wisdom grew, and many people sought him out for his advice, including Aelred of Rievaulx, Thomas Becket, and even Pope Alexander III. Godric was also a composer of music, the oldest surviving songs in English for which the original musical settings survive. He is, however, perhaps best remembered for his kindness toward animals, and many stories recall his protection of the creatures who lived near his home in the woods.

Godric's Garden and the Wild Deer

Now if one is intent too long upon one task, the mind in tedium very soon revolts against its undertaking: and so Godric, the man of God, would turn the energy of his mind to various activities, yet seldom did he suspend his soul from prayer. He had rooted up from the ground around his hermitage the undergrowth of the forest, and now he began upon the tree trunks that were left to graft in cuttings of fruit trees he had obtained from his visitors. Very skillful he was; he had made for himself a kind of enclosed orchard. In summer, when the tender shoots came to life again with green leaves, the branches he had grafted began to swell, and fragile sprays of green and young leaves appeared.

But the unaccustomed sweetness of them was tempting to the wild things of the woods, and they began greedily to nibble this strange new greenness. They would nip off the sprays of the apple boughs and gnaw the tender juicy bark, while scattering with their hooves the young saplings. Not a single tree of those Godric had grafted with so much care did these wild creatures of the forest allow to come to maturity.

So one day, coming out of his hermitage, he saw a wild stag from the woods cropping the tender leaves of his trees, scattering and spoiling the young growth. Approaching the creature, Godric bade it with a crook of his finger not to run away from that spot but to wait till he got there, without stirring.

Oh strange and stupendous mystery! The stag, this wild thing of the woods who knew no discretion, understood the will of the man of God from his gesture alone, and standing still, he began trembling all over, as if he knew he had offended the soul of the man of God. His extreme tremor and fear struck Godric's heart, and he checked his anger and the blows he had meant to inflict. The stag dropped on his knees as Godric came nearer and bowed his head, to ask pardon as best he could for his bold trespass. Godric ungirt his belt and put it around the neck of the kneeling animal. Then he led him beyond the bounds of the orchard, and there releasing him, told him to go free and wander wherever he wanted.

The Irksome Hare
Versus Godric's Concern for the Poor

Godric had planted vegetables in his garden to feed the poor, but a hare used to stealthily devour them. The holy man put up with the damage for a long time, but finally, his patience ran out. When the track of the hare's paws gave her away, Godric followed the thief. She turned in headlong flight, but he ordered her to stop.

The poor little creature did stop and waited in trembling and alarm for the arrival of her pursuer. The saint caught her and ordered, "See to it that neither you nor any of your acquaintance come to this place again; nor dare to encroach on what was meant for the needs of the poor."

Then, Godric tied a bundle of vegetables on the hare's shoulders and sent her off with a hearty meal for later consumption.

The Gentleness of Godric's Heart

The gentleness of the saint's heart was not only reflected in his kindness to people but also in his wise solicitude for the very reptiles and creatures of the earth. In winter, when all about was frozen in the cold, he would go out barefoot. Then, if he came upon any animal helpless with the misery caused by the cold, he would cuddle it under his armpit or in his bosom to warm it. Many times would the kind Godric go looking under the thick hedges or tangled patches of briars, and if he happened to find a creature that had lost its way or been harmed by the harshness of the weather so that it was tired or half dead, he would recover it with all the healing art he had.

If anyone in his service had caught a bird or little beast in a snare or a trap or a noose, as soon as he found it, he would snatch the animal from their hands and let it go free in the fields or the woods. Many times, his followers would hide their captive spoils under a corn measure or a basket or some other secret hiding place; but even so they could never deceive Godric or keep it hidden from him. Often, without saying a thing, despite the protestations and disavowals of the captors, he would go straight to the place where the creatures had been hidden. While the others stood by crimson-faced with fear and confusion, the holy man would lift the small creatures out from where they were hidden and set them free.

So, too, he would take in hares and other beasts fleeing from huntsmen and let them sleep with him in his hut. When all was safe once more, he would send the animals away to their familiar haunts. Many times, the creatures of the forest would run away from the huntsmen who lay in wait for them and take shelter in the safety of Godric's hut. They knew that a sure and safe refuge was provided for them there.

13

Ita of Killeedy

January 15 feast day

ITA (ALSO KNOWN AS ITE OR IDE) IS, AFTER Brigit, the most famous of Irish female saints. Her hagiographer even described her as "a second Brigit." A sixth-century abbess, Ita founded a monastery in Country Limerick at Killeedy (which means "cell—or church—of Ita"). She came from the highly-respected clan of the Deisi, whose family raised horses, which Ita cared for as a child.

While she loved her family and the animals, when she became a young woman, Ita discerned her calling as that of being a nun. Her father was resistant, but eventually, with the help of her mother and her own prayers, she was able to get his permission. Ita then left home and settled at the foot of Sliabh Luchra.

Other women from neighboring clans soon joined her. There she founded a monastic school for the education of boys, one of whom was Brendan of Clonfert. Tradition says the two became soul friends. Saint Brendan once asked Ita what were the three works most pleasing to God, and the three works most displeasing to God. Ita answered, "Three things that please God most are true faith in God with a pure heart, a simple life with a grateful spirit, and generosity inspired by charity. The three things that most displease God are a mouth that hates people, a heart harboring resentment, and confidence in wealth." Saint Brendan and all who were there, hearing that advice, glorified God in his chosen one.

Ita had many students, besides Brendan, and she is called the "Foster Mother of the Saints of Erin." Besides her significant mentoring, she is associated with competence in healing, guided as shamans are by dreams. Ita was also a powerful female confessor in the early Celtic Christian community, one who was not afraid of giving penances—and yet at the same was especially compassionate and forgiving. She also continued to be a lover of animals, not only horses but a special mule.

Ita's Qualities as a Child and Her Dream

Ita performed many miracles while she was yet a small child, and when she could speak and walk, she was prudent, generous, and mild toward everyone, human and animal alike. She consistently attempted to overcome evil and always did what she could to promote good.

One night when she was sleeping, Ita saw an angel of the Lord approach her and give her three precious stones. When she awoke, she did not know what that dream signified, and she had a question in her heart about it. Then an angel appeared to her and said, "Why are you wondering about that dream? These three precious stones you saw being given to you signify the coming of the Blessed Trinity to you, Creator, Son, and Holy Spirit. Always in your sleep and vigils the angels of God and holy visions will come to you, for you are a temple of God, in body and soul." After saying this, the angel left her.

A Rich Man's Desire for Red and White Colts

One time a rich man of the world came to Ita, knowing of her knowledge of horses, and said to her, "I ask you, holy one of God, that my mares will bear colts this year with red coloring and white heads."

Ita replied, "That is not in my limited power to do; it is for God to use the Earth's elements as God wishes."

Then the rich man asked her to intercede for him with God, saying, "As the Creator and Son and Holy Spirit, the triune and one God of Heaven and Earth, of sea and of all humans, who gave colors to Nature, clothes, and animals too, pray that this God will make the colors of my colts, as I desire."

Moved by his faith and his persistence, Ita said to him, "Since you believe this in God, so will your colts be this year as you wish."

The rich man went off delighted with that prophecy. And all happened to him as Ita had said.

Ita's Special Donkey

Ita was the proud owner of a very special donkey. All the milk that was used in her convent was brought there by the donkey every day from the dairy on the northern slope of a hill called Seeconglass, located four miles southwest of Killeedy. One day, as the beast was passing through a nearby town with his accustomed burden, a cruel-hearted man attacked him with dogs. The donkey, fleeing from his pursuers, jumped across the river that flows by the townland, leaving the imprints of his hoofs on a ledge of rock. Those marks can still be seen today. When Saint

Ita saw the donkey on his arrival, all torn and bleeding, in her anger she cursed the place where the outrage was committed.

Another time, while Ita was out riding her donkey, his leg became lame by stepping on a thorn on the road. When she saw her poor animal had begun to limp, she stopped immediately and removed the thorn from the donkey's hoof. This very thorn, then, grew into a tree whose thorns turned downwards and were therefore innocuous, not troubling any creatures thereafter.

14

Kevin of Glendalough

June 3 feast day

KEVIN STANDS AT THE FOREFRONT OF THE great company of Irish saints. One of Ireland's abbots of a monastery who was not a bishop but an ordinary priest, he was born sometime in the sixth century in the province of Leinster. As was true for many young people in the Middle Ages, including Hildegard of Bingen and the Venerable Bede, Kevin, at the age of seven was sent to a monastery to be educated by monks.

When he decided to be ordained, he wanted to live as a hermit, however, rather than remain in a monastic community. An angel, it is said, led him to a location in the Valley of the Two Lakes, near Glendalough, where he lived for seven years, clad only in animal skins and sleeping on a stone at the water's edge.

Considering the numerous stories about animals that are recorded in his *Life* and his obvious love of them, it is no wonder that he chose not to eat any meat. He lived, instead, on a frugal vegetarian diet of only nuts, berries, and herbs.

His reputation for holiness eventually attracted other monks, who begged Kevin to leave his solitary life and be their spiritual leader. They built the monastery at Glendalough, which eventually became a monastic city, whose ruins are still viewed today by pilgrims and tourists alike.

Kevin's love of animals led the local people to recognize his abilities as a veterinarian, and they brought sick animals to him, many of whom seemed to be miraculously cured by his touch. So many legends are told about his great love of Nature that he is often called the Irish Saint Francis of Assisi. Stories about him suggest that he and his community provided sanctuary in their monastery to both wild and tame creatures. The most famous story is his compassion for a mother blackbird, revealing his patience, gentleness, and stamina.

Kevin, the Hermit, and the Helpful Otter

After Kevin was ordained, an angel told him to go into the deserted glen. As he was setting out, the angel came to guide him to the crags on the western side of Glendalough's two lakes. There, he had no food but the nuts of the forest, the herbs of the earth, and freshwater for drinking. He did not even have a cell in which to live, but he would often go to the crag and to a cave there (known today as "Kevin's Bed"), and he would pray long and fervently to God.

For seven years, he followed this solitary routine, far from the companionship of others. One time, after Kevin had been in his place of solitude all night, he waded into the lake, as was his custom. As he was reciting his psalms, the book fell into the lake and sank to into the depths.

An angel came and said, "Do not grieve."

Soon an otter swam up from the bottom of the lake with Kevin's book in his mouth and gave it to Kevin. Not a line nor letter was blotched or blotted. The angel then told him to return to society to teach and preach the word of God, and not to hide himself any longer.

Kevin's Compassion for a Blackbird

All his life, Kevin was accustomed to spending every Lent in a wattled hut, with a grey flagstone under him as a bed. His only food was the music of the angels. Living in this way, he would spend six weeks in silence and prayer.

One Lent, a blackbird came from the woods to his hut and hopped on his palm as he prayed with his hand stretched out. Kevin kept his hand in that position, so that the blackbird could build its nest in it.

An angel came to visit Kevin and ordered him to stop his Lenten penance and return to society once more.

But Kevin refused. "It is no great thing for me to bear this pain of holding my hand under the blackbird for the sake of heaven's King," Kevin said, "for upon the Cross of suffering Jesus bore every pain on behalf of Adam's offspring."

"Come out of the hut," the angel insisted.

"I will not come," said he. He remained there holding the blackbird until she had hatched her brood of chicks.

Kevin Saves a Wild Boar

Another time, some hunters were hunting a wild boar, with their dogs in hot pursuit. As soon as the boar perceived the dogs near him, he set off down the slope of the glen to seek

Kevin's protection. Kevin protected the boar and commanded the dogs to stop following him.

Immediately, the dogs' paws stuck to the ground, so they could not move from that spot in any direction. Shortly after this, when the hunters came into Kevin's presence, they found their dogs fastened to the ground and the boar under Kevin's protection. They were astonished and filled with wonder at this miracle. Humbly and penitently, they asked Kevin to release their dogs, and then they promised Kevin they would never again pursue this boar.

So Kevin let the boar run to the forest, and the name of God was glorified. Kevin was like this all his life, working miracles until he died at an advanced age of a hundred and twenty-nine years.

15

Maedoc of Ferns

January 31 feast day

MAEDOC WAS BORN ABOUT 558 IN IRELAND on an island in County Davan. He is considered the founder of Irish monasteries at Fern in County Wexford, at Drumlane in Country Cavan, and Rossinver in County Leitrim. Maedoc is said to have been educated at Saint David's school in Wales, and tradition has it that David and Maedoc were very close friends, with David dying in the arms of his friend and former pupil.

Clearly, Maedoc had, like the other Celtic saints, a great capacity for making friends. Besides David, Maedoc had close ties with Molaise of Devenish (probably his closest friend), Columcille (a colleague), Ita of Killeedy, and even Brigit of Kildare. Besides being a good soul friend, the image of Maedoc that emerges in his hagiography is that of a powerful saint with a strong intuition and a great sensitivity toward those in pain.

He is named, as many Native Americans are, after an aspect of Nature: "son of star," a poetic title of honor. He is portrayed in the stories as close to Nature and a friend of many kinds of animals, landing back in Ireland after his schooling in Wales with hives of bees. He protected a stag being pursued by hounds, but he seems to have especially enjoyed the company of wolves. Perhaps he even danced with them!

Trees Falling and a Stag Protected

Maedoc and Molaise were comrades who loved each other very much. One day, they sat praying at the foot of two trees. "Ah, Jesus!" they cried, "is it your will that we should part, or that we should remain together until we die?" Then one of the two trees fell to the south, and the other to the north. "By the fall of the trees," they said, "it is clear that we must part." Then they told each other goodbye and kissed each other affectionately. Maedoc went to the south, and built a noble monastery at Ferns in the center of Leinster; Molaise went north to Lough Erne, where he built a fair monastery at Devenish.

Another day when Maedoc was praying deep in the forest, he saw a stag pursued by hounds. The stag stopped by him, and Maedoc threw the corner of his cloak over the stag's horns to protect it from the hounds. When the dogs came running by, they could neither see nor smell the stag. After they had gone, the animal ran for safety back into the forest

Maedoc Walks on Water and Shows Compassion for Wolves

One day when Maedoc was walking by the ocean with his comrades, he said to them, "I am sorry that I did not ask my master, David, who he thought should be my soul friend in Ireland."

His disciples began to prepare a ship, so that Maedoc could return to Wales to speak with David, but the boatmen were not willing to return to Wales. So Maedoc leapt out of the boat and walked from wave to wave until an angel met him.

"You need no soul friend but the God of the Elements," the angel said, "for the Holy One understands the thoughts and secrets of every person."

So Maedoc built a church in that place called Oakwood Hermitage, and he settled there with his disciples. The brothers had two cows and a calf in the community. One day Maedoc was alone in his cell when he saw some wolves approaching. They circled him gently, and he understood that they were asking for food. He was moved to compassion for them and gave the calf to them to eat.

But one of the brothers said to him, "Maedoc, the cow will not give milk without the calf."

Maedoc said to him, "Bend your head toward me so that I may bless it; for when the cows see you, they will give their milk obediently to you."

And so it was that whenever the cows saw the head of that brother, they would lick it and they "loved him like a calf" and give their milk to him.

The Starving Mother Wolf and the Miracle of a Loaf and a Fish

On another occasion, when Maedoc came to the monastery named Shanbo at the foot of the hill called Mount Leinster, he met a mother wolf on the road. She was wretched, weak, and starving. She came up to him gently as if seeking his attention.

Maedoc asked a lad who had joined him on the road whether he had any food he could give the wolf. The boy said he had only one loaf and a piece of fish. Maedoc took this from him and gave it to the wolf, who hungrily ate the food.

The boy was disturbed at seeing this and told the saint he was afraid of what his master would do to him for losing the food he was carrying.

Maedoc said, "Bring me some of the leaves of the forest"

The boy did as he had been told. Then Maedoc blessed the foliage, and it was turned into a loaf and a fish, which he gave to the lad, making both wolf and lad happy.

16

Melangell of North Powys

May 27 feast day

CELTIC MISSIONARIES AND WANDERING monks brought Christianity to many parts of Europe in the early Middle Ages, from lands such as Ireland, Brittany, and Wales to Italy and other parts of the Continent. Some of them came to evangelize, others to minister to the pastoral needs of the Irish who had already settled there. The Celts were known for their wandering and later for going on numerous pilgrimages to holy sites. As the medieval writer, Walafrid Strabo (c. 808–849), said, "The custom of traveling to foreign lands has now become almost second nature to them." Some of these Celts traveled simply seeking solitude.

Saint Melangell, the daughter of an Irish prince who lived in the early seventh century, was one of those long-ago Celts in search of a solitary life. Apparently, the only reason for her travel to Wales from Ireland was to find a quiet place to pray. Little is known about her except that when a local prince was out hunting rabbits with his dogs, this saintly woman protected one of the poor rabbits by hiding it beneath her dress. Because of her compassion, the prince made her, as the following stories show, a wonderful gift, and she remained in that place for thirty-seven years.

Because of her protection of rabbits, she became known as the patron saint of hares and other small animals. Her site in Wales, Pennant Melangell, is today as popular a place of pilgrimage as it was in medieval times. Anglican Canon A.M. Allchin calls her site one of the "thin places" where there is "the intersection of the timeless with time, where God's peace and eternity make their presence felt." Today Saint Melangell is also identified as the patron saint not only of small animals in Wales but all of Nature.

A Royal Hunt

In Powys, there was once a certain most illustrious prince by the name of Brychwel Ysgithrog. This man was the Earl of Chester, who at that time lived in the town of Pengwern Powys, which means in Latin "the head of Powys marsh." Now that very same noble prince gave his home for the use of God as an act of almsgiving, both by his own free will and out of a sense of religious duty, making a perpetual grant of it for his own sake and for the sake of his heirs.

One day in the year of our Lord 604, this prince went hunting in a certain place called Pennant, in the principality of Powys. When the prince's hunting dogs came upon a hare, they pursued it. The prince too gave chase until he came to a thicket of brambles that was large and full of thorns. In this thicket, he found a woman of beautiful appearance who, given up to divine contemplation, was praying with the greatest devotion. Meanwhile, the hare was lying boldly and fearlessly under the hem of her garments, her face toward the dogs.

Then the prince cried, "Get it, hounds, get it!" But the more he shouted, urging them on, the further the dogs retreated. Howling, they fled from the little animal.

Finally, the prince, altogether astonished, asked the woman how long she had lived on her own on his lands, in such a lonely spot. In reply, the woman said she had not seen a human face for the past fifteen years. Then he asked her who she was, her place of birth and origins. In all humility, she answered that she was the daughter of King Jowchel of Ireland and that "because my father had intended me to be the wife of a certain great and generous Irishman, I fled from my native soil and with God leading me, came here in order that I might serve God and the immaculate Virgin with my heart and pure body until my dying day." When the prince asked her name, she replied that her name was Melangell.

A Sanctuary Given in Melangell's Name

Then the prince, considering in his innermost heart the flourishing though solitary state of the woman, said: "O most worthy virgin Melangell, I find that you are a handmaid of the true God and a most sincere follower of Christ. Therefore, because it has pleased the highest and all-powerful God to give refuge, for your merits, to this little wild hare with safe conduct and protection from the attack and pursuit of these savage and violent dogs, I give and present to you most willingly these my lands for the service of God. I do so that they may be a perpetual asylum, refuge, and defense in honor of your name, excellent woman. Let neither king nor prince seek to be so rash or bold toward God that they presume to drag away any man or woman who has escaped here, desiring to enjoy protection in these your lands, as long as they in no way contaminate or pollute your sanctuary or asylum. But, on the other hand, if any wrongdoer who enjoys the protection of your sanctuary shall set out in any direction to do harm, then the independent abbots of your sanctuary, who alone know of their crimes, shall ensure, if they find them in that place, that the culprits be released and handed over to the Powys authorities to be punished." After the prince had told her this, that place called Pennant Melangell became a perpetual sanctuary—a refuge and safe haven for the oppressed, humans and animals alike.

The virgin Melangell, who was so very pleasing to God, led her solitary life for thirty-seven years in this very same place. And the wild rabbits and hares surrounded her every day of her life, just as if they had been tame or domesticated animals. With the aid of Divine mercy, she also performed miracles and various other signs for those people who, with an inner motion of their hearts, called upon her help and the grace of her favor. Melangell also worked to establish and instruct certain virgins who joined her, that they might persevere and live in a holy and modest manner in the love of God, doing nothing else by day and by night.

17

Modomnoc of Ossory

February 13 feast day

THE ORIGINAL CELTIC NAME OF THIS HOLY man was Domnoc, to which was added, as happened with Irish saints who were held in high affection, the word "mo," meaning "my, "little," "dear"; hence, the name Domnoc was changed to Modomnoc. This saint was an Irish missionary from present-day County Kilkenny who lived in the first half of the sixth century. At some point, he left Ireland to train for the priesthood with the famous Saint David at Menevia in Wales.

All those who resided in the monastic community there were expected to share in the manual work as well as the study and worship. Modomnoc's assignment was to care for the bees that were kept both for their honey and the production of mead. One of the best-known stories about him concerns his work as a beekeeper, especially his apparent ability to converse with them.

This folklore custom is called "telling the bees," and it is said to ensure that bees not feel any offense due to exclusion from family affairs, and so will remain with the hive. According to tradition, if a beekeeper didn't tell the bees of a wedding, a birth, or a death in the family, they would be "put into mourning," and a penalty would be paid; the bees might leave their hive, stop producing honey, or die. This custom of conversing with bees has been recognized in England, Ireland, Wales, Germany, Netherlands, France, Switzerland, and even the United States. It is artistically depicted in Charles Napier Hemy (1841–1917) in his painting, *Telling the Bees*, and poetically described in a poem by John Greenleaf Whittier (1807–1892), "Telling the Bees."

Because of Modomnoc's care for his bees and his loving attention to talking with them, he became known, along with Saint Gobnait, as the patron saint of bees and beekeepers. Bees were highly valued by the early church fathers too, such as Saints Ambrose and John Chrysostom; the latter said,

"The bee is more honored than other animals, not because she labors, but because she labors for others." Modomnoc may very well have been aware of that saying. In the ninth century, Óengus the Culdee wrote: "In a little boat, from the east, over the pure-colored sea, my Domnoc brought the gifted race of Ireland's bees." Modomnoc died sometime around the year 550.

Modomnoc "Telling the Bees"

When Modomnoc was given charge of the bees, he planted the kinds of flowers best loved by them in a sheltered corner of the monastery garden. He talked to the bees as he worked among them, and they buzzed around his head in clouds as if they were responding. He would walk among the hives in the evening and talk to them, and the bees, for their part, would fly out of the hives to greet him. He was never stung by them.

When the time came for Modomnoc to return to Ireland, three times the bees followed him in a great swarm and settled on the mast of the boat he was in. Saint David perceived this unusual occurrence and interpreted it to be a good omen. He therefore allowed Modomnoc to bring the bees to Ireland.

When he landed, Modomnoc built a church at a place called Bremore in County Dublin, and here he established the bees in a garden just like the one they had in Wales. He went on to serve God in the western part of the kingdom of Ossory, founding monasteries on the County Cork Coast.

18

Ninian of Whithorn

September 16 feast day

NINIAN IS SAID TO HAVE LIVED FROM 362 TO 432, and he is considered to be the first apostle in Scotland, where he preached the gospel some time before Columcille arrived at Iona. He was the son of a converted chieftain of the Cumbrian Britons, studied at Rome, was ordained a priest, and then was consecrated as a bishop.

Returning to evangelize his native Britain, he built a monastery at Whithorn in Galloway, on the southwestern coast of Scotland, which came to be known as Candida Casa (the

White House), evidently because of its white stone. Ninian and his monks used it as a base for their missionary work among the Picts in Scotland and Celts in Ireland. Our earliest authority on Ninian is Bede the Venerable (672–735), the first English historian, who wrote about the saint some three hundred years after Ninian's death. More details of Ninian's life are provided by Aelred of Rievaulx (c. 1110–1167), who had been brought up at the court of King David I of Scotland.

The Prayer of Encirclement for the Protection of Animals

It sometimes pleased the most holy Ninian to visit his flocks and the huts of his shepherds. He had gathered the sheep for the use of the monks, the poor, and pilgrims, and he wanted the beasts to be beneficiaries of his blessing. Therefore, when all the animals were gathered into one place, the servant of the Lord raised his hand and commended them all to the Divine protection. He walked around the flock, using his staff to draw a circle to enclose the animals, commanding that all within that space should that night remain under God's protection.

Having done all this, the man of God turned aside to rest for the night at the house of a certain honorable matron. When, after refreshing their bodies with food and their minds with the word of God, all had gone to sleep, certain thieves ventured near. Seeing that the cattle were neither enclosed by wall nor protected by hedges, they looked to see if anyone was watching who might resist their plans. When they saw that all was silent—no voice or bark or sound of movement—they rushed in and crossed the boundary the saint had fixed around the sheep. But the Divine power was present to resist the ungodly, casting them down. Filled with holy power, the ram rushed upon the men in fury, and striking at the leader of the thieves, threw him down. The fierce animal then pierced the man's belly with his horns, killing him. The other thieves discovered they were unable to leave the circle drawn around the flock. They cowered together there, filled with terror.

Meanwhile, the saint, having woken from his sleep and finished the solemn service of prayer, went outside and found the man lying dead among sheep. Ninian moved with compassion, and turning to God, he begged that life be restored to the thief. Nor did he stop crying tears and begging God's help.

Then, truly, the power of Christ, because of the merit of the saint, restored to life the dead robber. Meanwhile his fellow thieves, still enclosed within the circle the saint had made, cast themselves with fear and trembling at Ninian's knees, begging his pardon. The saint then gave them his blessing, after chiding them for their evil plans, and granted them permission to depart.

19

Petroc of Padstow

June 4 feast day

PETROC OF PADSTOW IS CONSIDERED
Cornwall's most famous saint. No definite dates are given
for his birth and death, however, other than general reference
to his living in the sixth century. Most likely he was born in
south Wales. His hagiography says that Petroc then studied in
Ireland for twenty years before coming to Cornwall, landing at
Haylemouth. From there he went to Lanwethinoc, now called
Padstow, where he founded a monastery. Padstow (named
after him: Petroc's Stow: the church of Saint Petroc) was the

principal center of his activities. About thirty years later, the holy man founded another monastery at Little Petherick.

Like many of the Celtic saints, Petroc seems to have preferred the solitary life. He lived as a hermit on Bodmin Moor, where he had built a cell for himself by the river. Near the cell, another monastery housed the twelve comrades who had accompanied him there.

Petroc died while on a visit to his monasteries, but his body was buried at Padstow. Like many Celtic saints, Petroc had a special affinity with wild animals, and he is often portrayed with a stag as his emblem—in memory of the one whom he sheltered from hunters. Petroc even healed a great dragon, surely another creature who merited the saint's compassion.

In the Wilderness, Petroc Protects a Fleeing Stag

In Cornwall, Petroc appointed Father Peter as prior; Peter was a most religious man whom Petroc himself had received into the faith. Petroc then departed for the desert, taking with him only twelve companions whom he had chosen to dwell with him in the wilderness among the valleys of the mountains and in hiding place in the rocks.

On a certain day, when the servant of God was praying alone in a place where he often prayed, he saw a stag appear in the distance. The animal was fleeing toward him as fast as he could go, pursued by the huntsmen of a rich man named Constantine and his loudly barking dogs. The saint, moved by compassion, protected the stag from being hurt.

When Constantine heard from his huntsmen what had happened, he was so full of wrath that he would have hit the servant of God with his sword. Suddenly, however, he was struck with paralysis, unable to move hand or foot, until he sought pardon from the saint. Petitioned by the soldiers, Petroc, through his prayers, healed the man. He then taught Constantine and his nineteen soldiers the Christian faith, and made them gentle and kind instead of fierce tyrants, worshippers of Christ

The Saint Heals a Dragon

So that the virtue of Petroc should be known even to "beasts that are not clean" (Genesis 7:2), when a great dragon who lived near the saint's cell in the wilderness was suffering from a piece of wood stuck in his right eye, he put aside his innate desire to harm people and hurried to the church where Petroc was praying.

Reclining his head on the outer threshold of the building, he lay there for three days, waiting for a miracle from God. By Petroc's command, the dragon was sprinkled with water mixed with dust from the pavement. Immediately, the wood was removed from his eye, and his sight was restored. Then, without creating any harm, he returned to his customary resting place.

20

Samthann of Clonbroney

December 19 feast day

ORN IN THE SECOND HALF OF THE SEVENTH
century, Samthann was an important abbess of the monastery at Clonbroney in County Longford, Ireland. According to one tradition, she was distantly related to Saint Patrick (who lived more than two hundred years before her). Like Saint Brigit, with whom she had much in common, many of Samthann's miracles concern food, and there are many accounts of her compassion and love for both animals and humans. We know little about her early life, except that she

was born in Ulster and that her distinguished foster father was a king of Ireland.

When Samthann entered the monastic community, her responsibilities included conducting the financial affairs of the monastery. This office evidently gave her opportunities to be generous to lepers and guests, pilgrims and penitents who visited there, as well as members of her own community. Her many other abilities are recounted in the stories about her. During her lifetime, she appeared in dreams to offer direction and advice; she had a capacity to heal those who came to her for help; she went into an ecstatic state while praying for the soul of a friend; and she multiplied food to satisfy a crowd of workers. Above all, Samthann is portrayed as a woman of prayer, someone who knocked frequently "at the doors of divine mercy." She died in 739.

The Power of Samthann's Prayers in Regard to Beasts, Wild and Tame

A certain monk once questioned Samthann about the way of praying. He wondered whether a person should pray lying down, sitting, or standing. She replied, "In *every* position, a person should pray." Another time, a monk asked Samthann's advice about going on pilgrimage to some distant country. She reminded him that God is as near to our homes as to any holy destination. "The Realm of Heaven is the same distance from every land, " she said, "for the Holy One is present everywhere."

According to tradition, Samthann's prayers were so powerful that on one occasion, she prayed a soul out of hell. By the power of her prayers, she also tamed the beasts in a pond near her monastery. They had previously caused havoc with people and the flocks, but after her prayer, they did no more harm.

On another occasion, a visiting monk lacked respect for Samthann's nuns and intended to sexually assault one of them. When the man crossed a river as he approached Samthann's monastery, a giant eel rose out of the water and wrapped itself around the man's waist. Although the man squirmed and struggled, he could not break free from the eel's grip—and so, with the eel still attached to him, the monk went to the monastery to beg Samthann's aid. When the shame-faced fellow confessed his lustful intentions and begged forgiveness, Samthann forgave him, prayed with him, and then returned the eel to its watery home.

This same saint—with the help of only one cow—once fed fifty guests until they were completely satisfied. At the time she had nothing else with which to feed them, but having prayed, the holy virgin milked the cow and drew forth enough milk to quench the thirst of that exact number of people.

Conclusion

"WHAT IS MORE WONDERFUL THAN THE incomparable tremendous story?" an Irish monk wrote some thousand years ago. He clearly knew the power of stories to nourish the soul, to strengthen the heart, and to influence a person's behavior. Celtic hagiographers knew this too, and in telling the stories of their saints they sought to teach lessons. One of these lessons is the reality that humans and animals are all related to one another, and that we are meant to enjoy each other's company, as well as alleviate each other's pain.

The *Lives* of these Celtic saints constitute the largest body of hagiographies of any group in Christian history that have so many animal stories included in them. While Native American and Hawaiian peoples, as well as certain

Asian spiritual traditions, have stories about animals, only the Celtic saints have so many references to them as fellow creatures. This sense of kinship was an intrinsic aspect of Celtic Christian spirituality that affected not only those living in Celtic lands but also significantly influenced later saints who were raised in geographical areas on the Continent ministered to by Irish missionaries.

The multi-talented German mystic Hildegard of Bingen (1098–1179), for example, expressed her belief in the unity of all creation in the theology of greenness she developed as a theologian and writer. In the hagiography she wrote on Saint Disibod, the Irish missionary and founder of her first monastery, she specifically showed her appreciation of the Irish contribution to her life.

Francis of Assisi (1181–1226), as mentioned earlier, lived in a part of Italy where Christianity had been brought by the great Irish missionary, Saint Columban, and as a pilgrim, Francis visited Columban's tomb in Bobbio. The numerous animal stories associated with Francis, and his attitude of compassion toward animals and birds as sisters and brothers reflect the spirituality of the Celtic saints. In particular, his famous "Canticle of the Sun" expresses his love of all creatures, great and small. (Francis saw the entire cosmos, sun, moon, and all the stars as brothers and sisters too.)

Joan of Arc (1412–1431), born in the part of France originally populated by the ancient Celts and raised in the tiny village of Domremy visited by the Irish, spoke of a "Fairy Tree" where she and other children used to play when she was growing up. Joan's grandmother also told her stories of fairies. Joan, of course, epitomizes a Celtic shaman who heard voices and saw visions. She was also a Celtic female warrior, something which, while unusual in her own day, was common among early Celts. She was visited by saints, two of whom, Catherine and Michael, were favorites of Celtic Christians. Her life was certainly a manifestation of what Carl Jung calls the collective unconscious that lived in her.

The stories in this book attest to the Celtic awareness, ancient and Christian, that all of life is interconnected. It seems that for Celtic Christians, one of the most significant criteria for sainthood was the compassionate treatment not only of human beings but of all Creation, especially our fellow creatures. Celtic hagiographers suggest to their readers that to be a holy person one must have this same type of relationship and awareness.

The stories told here allude to the sense of kinship the saints felt with animals, as well as their compassion toward them.

- Patrick saves a young deer from being slain by his own men.

- Brigit saves a hunted boar.

- Columcille manifests hospitality to a tired crane.

- Brendan recognizes a strange dog as a helpful guide and a whale as a place of shelter.

- Ciaran of Saighir welcomes a boar, a fox, a badger, a wolf, and a deer as his first monks.

- Kevin leaves his arms outstretched, giving a mother blackbird time for her chicks to hatch.

So many of the saints are portrayed as helping the hunted, protecting them from harm. This act of saving animals being pursued by hunting dogs is a common storyline in the *Lives* of the Celtic saints: Maedoc throws his cloak over a stag pursued by hounds; Melangell hides a hunted hare beneath her skirt; Petroc protects yet another fleeing stag.

Of all the saints, only Godric is portrayed as impatient with wild animals. His reason, we recall, was his objection to the animals eating from his garden when the food was for the poor. Even so, he was gentle as he led them away, putting up a fence to keep them out and being solicitous even toward snakes! And, the hagiographer reminds us, in winter, "when all about was frozen stiff in the cold, he would go out barefoot, and if he lighted on any animal helpless with misery of the cold, he would set it under his armpit or in his bosom to warm it. . . . And if anyone in his service had caught a bird or little beast in a snare or a trap or a noose, as soon as he found it he would snatch it from their hands and let it go free in the fields or the glades of the wood." Though impatient with some creatures, Godric obviously demonstrates an exceptional degree of compassion and love.

These are just a few of the things the saints did for animals. But the stories also show what animals did for them; the reciprocity that underlies so much *when we pay attention*—as the farmer does eventually with his pig in the movie, *Babe*.

- Ciaran of Clonmacnois had a fox who acted as a sort of mail carrier between him and another monk. He also had a stag that used to visit him and allow Ciaran to place his books on the stag's antlers while the saint read.

- Ciaran of Saighir, as already mentioned, had his monastery built with the help of animals "as if they had been his monks"—perhaps the first ever of lay oblates or consociates increasingly popular today.

- Colman's monastic inhabitants—a rooster, a mouse, and a fly—ministered to him. As we recall from the story, while the rooster acted as a sort of alarm clock, the mouse would also wake him by gnawing at his clothes or nibbling at his ear, and the third creature, a fly, would act as a marker on the page which he was reading, if Colman was called away.

Still other animals provided comfort and compassion to the saints.

- Otters ministered to Cuthbert by warming his cold feet with their breath, even drying him with their fur.

- A bear helped Gall build a fire.

- A white bird guided Brendan on his voyage to the Promised Land, and the whale, Jasconius, provided his back for Brendan's boat to rest on.

In effect, what all these stories reveal is that animals often became a significant part of the saints' daily lives, important members of the monastic community itself.

As we look back, then, over the stories of saints and creatures in fellowship, a pattern can be discerned already alluded to: one of *reciprocity* that transcends species differences so that all benefit in the circle of life. Kindness, compassion, and loving respect on the part of the saints elicit from their creature-partners trust, caring, and love—which, in turn, increases the happiness of everyone. We have but to recall the story of Columban, the great Irish missionary to France, Switzerland, and Italy, which tells how he would call to the creatures as he walked through the woods: "They would come at once to his call, and he would stroke them with his hand and caress them; and the wild things and the birds would leap and frisk about him for sheer happiness, jumping up on him as puppies jump on their masters." Even the squirrel "would come at his call from the high tree-tops, and the saint would take it in his hand and set it on his shoulder, and it would be running in and out of the folds of his cowl. . . ." The joy is certainly evident in this story, a happiness that is shared by the animals and the saint himself.

The question can be asked: did this sense of kinship translate into any of the early Celtic saints' dietary choices? Judging from the saints' lives, as well as certain Celtic monastic Rules, the evidence is mixed.

Columcille on Iona, as related earlier, evidently followed a vegan diet and expected his monks to do the same. Brendan was a vegan who "from the time of his ordination to the priesthood tasted nothing in which the spirit of life drew support from flesh." David of Wales, according to his hagiography, rejected wine, beer, and everything intoxicating, leading "a blessed life for God on bread and water only." The daily diet of another saint, Finnian of Clonard (470–549), consisted of "a bit of barley-bread and a drink of water," but on holy days "he would eat a slice of wheat bread and piece of broiled salmon, and drink a full cup of clear mead or of ale."

Many later monks seem to have followed these early monks' examples. In the latter half of the eighth century, Maelruain (d. 792), the founder of the Celi De reform movement, allowed only vegetables, a dry egg, cheese, and an occasional morsel of fish—but no meat—and no beer for most meals at his monastery of Tallaght, outside of Dublin. "From the moment of his initiation into the clerical state," his Rule of Tallaght said, "a man did not eat the fat of bacon, or mutton, or venison or the meat of any other animal"—not even at the great celebration of Easter. At times, however, a monk could "content himself with salmon" (understandable, since it was the fish associated, for the Celts, with wisdom).

In their admiration for the ascetic desert monks who had preceded them, early Celtic monks seem to have followed a highly restrictive diet. Some were vegan, while many others followed a vegetarian diet in which fish was allowed occasionally. (Celtic monastic pescatarians?!) Whether their vegetarian or vegan diets were at all related to a respect for and compassion toward animals is difficult to know, but surely some, like Columcille and his decision to not allow any animals to be killed or eaten on Iona, did so as the result of their compassion and sense of interrelatedness—dimensions found in the stories of their saints.

Considering these stories of the saints, as well as their history of choices in their diets, what is it, then, that we might learn from them today in a world that is increasingly becoming more urbanized—and thus more removed from direct contact with Nature and animals, wild or domestic?

From Patrick's protection of innocent deer when others wanted to kill them, we might challenge people who consider the hunting of wild animals (as well as so-called "trophy" animals) as a "sport," encouraging them to find other forms of recreation that do not involve the killing of fellow creatures. From Brigit's concern for a terror-stricken boar and a flock of wild ducks, we might consider how animals are treated today in labs and factory farms, and the extreme cruelty and often prolonged suffering and terror they endure. From Columcille's decision that "the implement I bless will do no harm," we might work toward ending the slaughter of animals for food simply because we like the taste of meat. Maedoc's sympathy for a starving wolf might make us more attentive to the treatment of wolves today that is driving them toward extinction. Kevin's patient care for a blackbird's nest and Melangell's for rabbits may induce us to contribute to shelters for birds and animals of all kinds. Even Godric has something to teach us about the treatment of those who are perceived as invaders to our gardens, inviting us to, yes, perhaps set up fences but still to treat animals "kindly"—not destroying them for their simple and natural desire to share our abundance.

Above all, what the stories show is how much our fellow creatures can contribute to our lives without having to give up theirs, so that we can all experience, like Columban, the shared joy of partnership. In response to this renewed awareness of our kinship with them, we too might reorient our lives, as many of the Celtic monks did, by choosing different approaches to our consumption of food, asking whether it is necessary for us to choose a vegetarian, if not a vegan, diet.

All of this presupposes a new spirituality of holiness, different from that which has often been taught—and which increasing numbers of people, young and old, are rejecting, especially if raised in the Christian tradition. Instead of hearing that holiness is all about sexual continence and only a specific sexual orientation, the stories of the saints might remind us of the importance of developing an ethic of caring for Creation in all its wondrous diversity. Instead of preaching or being lectured on the importance of rules and respect for the hierarchy or elders, the example of the saints might rather teach the need for engaging in ministries of service and servant leadership. Instead of concentrating our attention on the wealthy and the privileged, the saints' lives might affirm the importance of attending to the poor, the neglected, the marginalized, and all who suffer, human and otherwise.

In the development of this "new spirituality," we might discover that it isn't really all that new! Jesus, when he walked the earth, saw God's love and compassion reflected in myriad ways, from the lilies of the field to the birds of the air, and especially in the lives of all who are suffering (cf. Luke 13:34, Matthew 6:26 ff). Jesus challenged his followers to incorporate that awareness into their daily lives. His life encourages the pursuit of loving all creatures great and small, beginning with the tiny, fragile, beautiful planet on which we all live. Christ's ministry was about alleviating suffering whenever he saw it, and he calls us still to do the same, to see his face in suffering humans like ourselves—but also to see, as the Anglican theologian Andrew Linzey recommends, "the face of the Crucified in the faces of suffering animals."

History shows, and these stories reveal, that the ancient Celts had a high regard for animals as teachers and guides, healers and soul friends. They considered animals in many ways equal to humanity, and in some ways superior in their awareness and sensitivities. The Celtic saints reflected that awareness in their lives and their spirituality. Their sense of kinship with all of creation, their awareness of the reciprocity and friendship that we can have with our fellow creatures, can inspire us to create modern-day lifestyles built around concern with the creatures that share our world.

The ninth-century anonymous author of "Pangur Bán," the poem about a cleric's cat that was mentioned in the introduction, concludes his poem with this stanza:

> *Practice every day has made*
> *Pangur perfect in his trade;*
> *I get wisdom day and night,*
> *Turning darkness into light.*

And so, may each of us, with the help of our animal teachers and guides, turn darkness into light, learning and sharing wisdom with all our fellow creatures.

Bibliography

Alexander, Dominic. *Saints and Animals in the Middle Ages.* Rochester, NY: Boydell Press, 2008.

Armstrong, Edward. *Saint Francis: Nature Mystic.* Berkeley: University of California Press, 1973.

Atherton, Mark. *Hildegard of Bingen: Selected Writings.* Penguin Books, 2001.

Barstow, Anne Llewellyn. *Joan of Arc: Heretic, Mystic, Shaman.* Lewiston, NY: Edwin Mellen Press, 1986.

Buechner, Frederick. *Godric.* New York: Harper Collins, 1980.

Carey, John, Herbert, Maire & O Riain, Padraig, eds. *Saints and Scholars: Studies in Irish Hagiography.* Dublin: Four Courts Press, 2001.

Chadwick, Nora. *The Age of the Saints in the Early Celtic Church.* London: Oxford University Press, 1961.

Charbonneau-Lassay, Louis. *The Bestiary of Christ.* New York: Parabola Books, 1991.

Charles-Edwards, T.M., *Early Christian Ireland.* Cambridge University Press, 2000.

Colgrave, Bertram, trans. *Two Lives of Saint Cuthbert.* Cambridge University Press, 1985.

Davies, Marion. *Sacred Celtic Animals.* Berks, England: Capall Ban Publishing, 1998.

Davies, Oliver, trans. *Celtic Spirituality.* New York: Paulist Press, 1999.

Duckett, Eleanor. *The Wandering Saints.* London: The Catholic Book Club,1959.

Dumville, David, ed. *Kathleen Hughes: Church and Society in Ireland, A.D. 400–1200.* London: Variorum Reprints, 1987.

Flower, Robin. *The Irish Tradition.* Oxford at Clarendon Press, 1947.

Follett, Westley. *Celi De In Ireland: Monastic Writing and Identity in the Early Middle Ages.* Woodbridge, UK: Boydell Press, 2007.

Ginnell, Laurence. *The Brehon Laws.* London: T. Fisher Unwin, 1896.

Gougaud, Dom Louis, OSB. *Christianity in Celtic Lands.* Four Courts Press, 1992.

___. *Modern Research with Special Reference to Early Irish Eclesiastical History.* Dublin: Hodges, Figgis & Co., 1929.

Green, Miranda. *Animals in Celtic Life and Myth*. London: Routledge, 1992.

___. *Symbol & Image in Celtic Religious Art*. London: Routledge, 1989.

Hood, A.B.E., ed. and trans. *St. Patrick: His Writings and Muirchu's Life*. London: Phillimore, 1978.

Jackson, Kenneth. *Studies in Early Celtic Nature Poetry*. Cambridge University Press, 1935.

Johnson, Elizabeth. *Ask the Beasts: Darwin and the God of Love*. London: 2014.

Jonas of Bobbio. *Life of St. Columban*. Charleston, SC: BiblioLife, LLC, n.d.

Kemmerer, Lisa. *Animals and World Religions*. Oxford University Press, 2011.

Knox, David Blake. *The Curious History of Irish Dogs*. Stillorgan, Ireland: New Island Books, 2017.

Linzey, Andrew. *Animal Gospel*. Louisville, KY: Westminster John Knox Press, 1998.

___. *Why Animal Suffering Matters*. Oxford University Press, 2009.

Low, Mary. *Cherish the Earth*. Glasgow: Wild Goose Publications, 2003.

Mac Coitir, Niall. *Ireland's Animals: Myths, Legends, & Folklore*. Cork, Ireland: Collins Press, 2010.

Matthews, John. *Celtic Totem Animals*. London: Connections Book Publishing, 2015.

McGinnis, Mark. *Buddhist Animal Wisdom Stories*. Boston: Weatherhill, n.d.

Meehan, Bridget Mary, and Oliver, Regina Madonna. *Praying with Celtic Holy Women*. Liguori, MO: Liguori/Triumph, 2003.

Meyer, Kuno. *Ancient Irish Poetry*. London: Constable, 1994.

Murphy, Gerard. *Saga and Myth in Ancient Ireland*. Dublin: At the Sign of the Three Candles, 1955.

Olmsted, Garrett. *The Gundestrup Cauldron*. Bruxelles: Collection Latomus, Vol. 162, 1979.

O Maidin, Uinseann. *The Celtic Monk: Rules and Writings of Early Irish Monks*. Kalamazoo, MI: Cistercian Publications, 1996.

O Meara, John, trans. *The Voyage of Saint Brendan*. Channel Islands: Colin Smythe Ltd., 1991.

O Riain, Padraig. *A Dictionary of Irish Saints*. Dublin: Four Courts Press, 2012.

Plummer, Charles. *Vitae Sanctorum Hiberniae*, Vol. I. London: Oxford University Press, 1810.

___. *Lives of Irish Saints*, Vol. II. London: Oxford University Press, 1968.

Roberts, Holly. *Vegetarian Christian Saints*. Anjeli Press, 2004.

Russack, Neil. *Animal Guides: In Life, Myth and Dreams*. Toronto: Inner City Books, 2002.

Salisbury, Joyce. *The Beast Within: Animals in the Middle Ages*. New York: Routledge, 1994.

Scott, Michael. *Irish Animal Tales*. Dublin: Mercier Press, 1989.

Schweitzer, Albert. *Civilization and Ethics*. London: Adam & Charles Black, 1946.

Sellner, Edward. *Stories of the Celtic Soul Friends: Their Meaning for Today*. New York: Paulist Press, 2004.

___. *The Celtic Soul Friend*. Notre Dame, IN: Ave Maria Press, 2002.

___. *Wisdom of the Celtic Saints: Revised and Expanded Edition*. St. Paul, MN: Bog Walk Press, 2006.

Skinner, John, trans. *The Confession of St. Patrick*. New York: Image Books, 1998.

Stokes, Whitley, trans. *Lives of Saints from the Book of Lismore*. Oxford: Clarendon Press, 1890.

Thom, Catherine. *Early Irish Monasticism: An Understanding of its Cultural Roots*. London: T&T Clark, 2007.

Trask, Willard. *Joan of Arc: In Her Own Words*. New York: Turtle Point Press, 1996.

Waddell, Helen, trans. *Beasts and Saints*. London: Constable and Company, 1934.

About the Author

E DWARD SELLNER IS PROFESSOR EMERITUS OF theology and spirituality at St. Catherine University in St. Paul, Minnesota, where he taught graduate and undergraduate courses for thirty-five years, as well as administered pastoral ministry, spiritual direction, and master's degree programs. A graduate of the University of Notre Dame, he is the author of numerous articles and books on Celtic spirituality, the history of Western monasticism, and animal theology. He is a Fellow of the Oxford Centre of Animal Ethics, Oxford, England. He is also a spiritual director, trained at the Jung Institute in Zurich, Switzerland.

Water from an Ancient Well

Celtic Spirituality for Modern Life

Pilgrimage Study Edition

A Fresh Look at Celtic Spirituality

This new version has more than 150 pages of previously unpublished material, including illustrated guides to Celtic pilgrimage sites, study questions, and updated research.

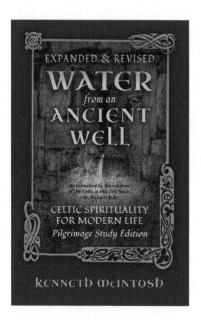

Using story, scripture, reflection, and prayer, Kenneth McIntosh offers us a taste of the living water that refreshed the ancient Celts, allowing them to perceive God as a living Presence in everybody and everything. This Earth-based and inclusive perspective suggests life-giving alternatives to modern faith practices, opening the door to a Christianity big enough to embrace the entire world.

The Celtic Book of Days

Ancient Wisdom for Each Day of the Year from the Celtic Followers of Christ

The ancient Celts found God's presence in each ordinary moment of the day. Everything they encountered revealed to them the presence of the sacred; each day was deep with meaning. Now you too can practice the Celts' faith, as you take a few moments to immerse yourself in their wisdom. These small daily moments of reflection and insight will open your heart to each day and all it holds.

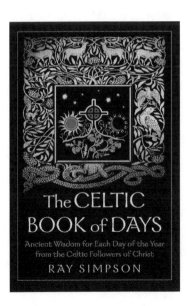

"In this splendid book of daily readings, Ray Simpson draws from scripture, liturgy, folklore, his knowledge of history, and the power of his own experience to weave a richly textured tapestry of insight, invocation, and invitation."

– Carl McColman, author of *Befriending Silence: Discovering the Gifts of Cistercian Spirituality* and *The Big Book of Christian Mysticism*

Sacred Soil
A Gardener's Book of Reflection

In these fifteen intimate essays, Melina Rudman explores the pain of loss and the joy of connection, all within the context of her garden. She writes of gardening as a spiritual practice, one that has the power to ground us in the seasons and cycles of Nature. Gardening, she says, plants us firmly in the circle of birth, life, and death, "smack dab in the middle of life's gore and glory." While gardening focuses on the world of touch and sight and scent, it also opens doors to deeper realities. It teaches us resilience; it shows us how to let go; it comforts our aching hearts; it leads us to repentance—and it offers us a conduit to the Divine.

*Spirit, I give thanks
that I am held in a great web
of Being,
where the energy of earth
and memory,
tree and thought, flower
and emotion,
are all knit together into You.*

Celtic Nature Prayers
Prayers from an Ancient Well

This prayerbook offers a Nature-focused collection based on ancient
Celtic prayers, weaving together words of hope and challenge.
Each prayer is an opportunity to connect personal faith with
environmental concerns. The prayers also work well as an opening
or closing for gatherings and meetings, to remind those present
to turn their hearts to the Earth. Using these Celtic patterns of
prayer, readers become rooted in an ancient tradition that has always
integrated spirituality with an awareness of the Earth. This Celtic
form of "green spirituality" creates a desperately needed twenty-
first-century pathway to
greater spiritual and practical
commitment to Nature.

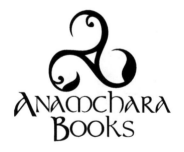

AnamcharaBooks.com

Made in the USA
Middletown, DE
01 April 2024

52408969R00125